Working Class Experiences of Social Inequalities in (Post-) Industrial Landscapes

Based on qualitative research among industrial workers in a region that has undergone deindustrialisation and transformation to a service-based economy, this book examines the loss of status among former manual labourers. Focus lies on their emotional experiences, nostalgic memories, hauntings from the past and attachments to their former places of work, to transformed neighbourhoods, as well as to public space. Against this background the book explores the continued importance of class as workers attempt to manage the declining recognition of their skills and a loss of power in an "established-outsider figuration". A study of the transformation of everyday life and social positions wrought by changes in the social structure, in urban landscapes and in the "structures of feeling", this examination of the dynamic of social identity will appeal to scholars of sociology, anthropology and geography with interests in post-industrial societies, social inequality, class and social identity.

Lars Meier is Professor for Sociology and Social Inequality at the Institute for Sociology, Goethe-Universität Frankfurt, Germany.

Cities and Society

Series editor: Chris Pickvance, Professor of Urban Studies, University of Kent, UK

This series welcomes books which contribute to a sociological understanding of the city. The following list of possible topics is illustrative, not exhaustive.

- The city as a place of unequal access to good public and private services (e.g. schools, parks, housing, jobs) and environments.
- How people respond to bad services and environments: (resignation, individual action, collective action): urban protest, urban conflict.
- Urban governance: urban politics as a means of reconciling conflicts; partnerships in theory and practice; decentralizing decision-making (who benefits).
- Urban infrastructure and its regulation (is private production and management compatible with public need?).
- The impact of post-socialist transition, welfare regimes, and gender regimes.
- Social divisions and stratification.
- Poverty and coping.
- Residential segregation and its effects.
- Religion and the city.
- Privacy, sociability and lifestyles.
- The city and space: imagining urban space, interaction in urban space, privatization and control of urban space.
- The city and public safety/personal security: personal, organizational and state perspectives.
- The sustainable city: its many meanings and steps (and obstacles) towards realising it.

Published titles in this series:

Brands and the City
Entanglements and Implications for Urban Life
Sonia Bookman

Transport, Transgression and Politics in African Cities
The Rhythm of Chaos
Edited by Daniel E. Agbiboa

Contentious Politics and the Welfare State
Squatting in Sweden
Dominika V. Polanska

For more information about this series, please visit: https://www.routledge.com/sociology/series/ASHSER1347

Working Class Experiences of Social Inequalities in (Post-) Industrial Landscapes

Feelings of Class

Lars Meier

Routledge
Taylor & Francis Group
LONDON AND NEW YORK

First published 2021
by Routledge
2 Park Square, Milton Park, Abingdon, Oxon OX14 4RN

and by Routledge
52 Vanderbilt Avenue, New York, NY 10017

Routledge is an imprint of the Taylor & Francis Group, an informa business

British Library Cataloguing-in-Publication Data
A catalogue record for this book is available from the British Library

Library of Congress Cataloging-in-Publication Data
A catalog record has been requested for this book

ISBN: 978-1-138-31217-3 (hbk)
ISBN: 978-0-367-77502-5 (pbk)
ISBN: 978-0-429-45840-8 (ebk)

Typeset in Times New Roman
by codeMantra

Contents

Figures and table

Figures

Table

Acknowledgments

This book was long in the making. Many people – friends, colleagues, students and family members – have accompanied me on the demanding journey to completion and I thank them for their support and inspiration. The book could not exist without the biographic narratives of the interviewees: I want to thank them for allowing me to collect their life stories. My book is based on data that I collected in the SPHERE project (7th framework programme of the EU, SSH8-5.2.01). I thank all project partners for their great cooperation and especially Markus Promberger for his support during SPHERE.

An earlier version of the book was accepted as a habilitation thesis at the Technische Universität Berlin. I thank Martina Löw, Helmuth Berking and Nina Baur for their kind and constant support and intellectual motivation during my bumpy route through academia.

We started our academic careers as four PhD students in Darmstadt and I am so happy that I could always count on you: thanks for this Sybille, Lars and Silke!

The book includes revised versions of previously published articles.

- A previous version of Chapter 4 appeared as (Meier 2016a) "Metalworkers' nostalgic memories and optimistic official representations of a transformed industrial landscape", *The Sociological Review* 64(4): 766–785.
- A previous version of Chapter 5 appeared as (Meier 2013a) "Encounters with haunted industrial workplaces and emotions of loss – Class-related senses of place within the memories of metalworkers", *Cultural Geographies* 20(4): 467–483.
- An earlier version of Chapter 6 appeared as (Meier 2017) "Transformations of public space and the limits of resistance in biographic narratives of workers", *Space and Culture* 20(2): 156–169.
- Chapter 7 appeared in a previous version as (Meier 2013b) "Everyone knew everyone: Diversity, community memory and a new established outsider figuration", *Identities* 20(4): 455–470.

- Chapter 8 was published in a slightly different form as (Meier 2016b) "'I am now a nobody' – Transformations of home and senses of belonging in the life narrative of a migrant worker in the industrial sector in Nuremberg", in Katie Walsh and Lena Näre (eds.), *Transnational Migration and Home in Older Age* (pp. 165–175). New York: Routledge.

I would like to thank the publishers and editors for permission to reuse my work. I am grateful to the series editor Chris Pickvance for the close reading of my manuscript and for the very helpful comments. Thanks to Lukas Watschko and to Nils Richterich for their help in formatting and revising the manuscript.

Most of all I thank Pia. Without you and your untiring support, intellectual inspiration and everything else, this book would not exist.

1 Introduction

> Just as the entire mode of existence of human collectives changes over long historical periods, so too does their mode of perception. The way in which human perception is organised – the medium in which it occurs – is conditioned not only by nature but by history.
>
> Walter Benjamin (2008 [1936]: 23)

Industrial areas, and the people living or working in these areas, have experienced enormous transformations, especially since the 1970s. These transformations manifest themselves not only in material structures, such as in the ruins of former factories (Edensor 2005a; Mah 2012; Storm 2014; Voiculescu and Jucu 2016), in newly established office buildings or in upgraded and gentrified working-class housing developments. Transformations also become apparent in everyday social encounters and interactions, such as in regions that have become socially more diverse (Vertovec 2007). It is known that economic and spatial transformations go hand in hand with a change in social structure. Yet the relevance of social transformations for everyday individual identity positioning in these areas remains largely unknown.

The transformations of the social structure and the growing social inequality in Germany have been frequently evidenced by social statistics.[1] I adopt a different perspective on the transformation of social inequality by showing how the latter is individually experienced and reproduced. The individual experience of social inequality is accompanied by daily identity-related repositionings in a local social structure. Social identities are dynamic and related to social structures. This means that transformations of the social structure are reflected in the individuals' changed social positions. Changes in the structures of social inequalities may therefore also be described as the individuals' identity-related repositionings in a social structure.

In this book, transformations are referred to as processes which have an effect on emotions at the subjective level. Raymond Williams' concept of "structures of feeling" (Williams 1965, 1977) explains this close relationship between transformation and the emotional individual.[2] He argues that objective structures, forms and values are "actively lived and felt" in the individuals' everyday lives (Williams 1977: 132), thereby relaying the "structures of feeling" between the individual and the social. I will show that there is also a relationship between social structure and individual emotions.

The "structures of feeling" are dynamic and not "fixed forms" (Williams 1977: 129); they are conceptualised as "social experiences in solution" (Williams 1977: 133). These current "structures of feeling" have not only been coined by hegemonic structures and ideologies, but by the past ("residual") and the future ("emergent"; Williams 1977: 121–127) simultaneously. Thus, transformations do not only become evident in the comparative retrospection on previous conditions, be it by studying historical sources or by demonstrating social statistical historical comparisons of time series analyses of unemployment or income distributions,[3] but they also become evident in the present time. This understanding of transformation allows us first of all to conceive of transformations not as comprehensive and absolute, and therefore, second, to be able to analyse transformations even in current narratives as well as in narrated biographical memories by interviewed industrial workers, and finally, to comprehend the individuals' social positions within a social structure as being dynamic, in that they are affected by any position changes, which also have a clear effect on their emotions.

I argue in favour of an analysis of social inequality conceived of as being dynamic, a dynamic of incomplete processes and changes in social positions within the social structure that have an emotional effect. Against this backdrop, I will point out the relevance of the long-neglected, often anachronistically appearing analytical category of class. The argument is that class is not only relevant in specific practices and in the availability of economic and social resources (Bourdieu 1984; Savage 2000), but also has a subjective emotional reality (Sennett and Cobb 1972; Sayer 2005; Kirk 2007; Walkerdine 2010), resulting in a "psychic landscape of class" (Reay 2005). From a sociological perspective I refer to emotions as social facts, which at the individual level manifest themselves in negative or positive emotional expressions. These are responses to the assessment of stimuli and situations and have themselves a structuring effect on the social setting (Gerhards 1988: 16). Individuals' social positions are accompanied by emotional experiences (Kemper 1978; Sayer 2005), which, as in the case of a loss of status, can be expressed through the feeling of shame (Neckel 1991).

In this introduction, I propose in a first step to understand biographical narratives and emotional descriptions of current visits to the locations as well as social encounters and practices as social positionings in the present – the time when narratives are presented. At the same time, the oftentimes nostalgia-laden narratives of industrial workers come to mind, framed as today's confrontation with the ghosts of the past (Gordon 2008). These narratives are not only backward-looking, but express a self-positioning based on present-day identities.

On this basis, I will show in a second step that in narrated memories, local references and thereby also the self-positioning in a local environment (transformed industrial landscapes) are relevant and that these, together with the "structures of feeling" approach, need to be taken into account.

In a third step it will become evident "that every person is fundamentally related to other people, and that every human individual is fundamentally a social being" (Elias 2001: 124)[4] and how individuals with their narrated memories therefore function as part of a figuration. Thus, the figuration approach lends itself to being able to take a specific analytical look at the process of power inequalities in the relationship between different social groups. Figurations have a processual nature and allow analysing changes in people's position in the social hierarchy, such as a changing local established-outsider figuration (Elias and Scotson 1965), as the narratives reveal.

The next paragraph in this introduction, which closes with an overview of the different book chapters, shows that the relevance of class in the interviewees' subjective experiences, emotions and narrated memories becomes evident as well.

Transformations: biographical narratives and social inequality

> Memory is life, always embodied in living societies and as such in permanent evolution, subject to the dialectic of remembering and forgetting, unconscious of the distortions to which it is subject, vulnerable in ways to appropriation and manipulation, and capable of lying dormant for long periods only to be suddenly reawakened. History, on the other hand, is reconstruction, always problematic and incomplete, of what is no longer. Memory is always a phenomenon of the present, a bond tying us to the eternal present; history is the representation of the past.
>
> (Nora 1996: 3)

Biographical memories, as they have been recorded for this book in form of biographical interviews (see Chapter 2), are a problem if one intends to use them as historical data sources, because biographical memories are not "objective" retrospections on people's own lives. Instead, they represent a "biographical illusion" as Pierre Bourdieu puts it (Bourdieu 2004 [1986]), due to forgetting, to new conceptualisation or even to unintentionally inventing experiences. In such interviews, past and future are set into a suitable relationship and single events are included, converting one's life into a narrative story line (Ricoeur 1991). So why should a sociological research project work with such an uncertain data source?

To answer this requires a change of perception. This book is not about a historical retrospection and analysing how things actually were in earlier days or in which ways things specifically changed. Rather, the narrated memories are understood and analysed as personal social positionings in the present. Following this argument, I prefer to use the term "life story" instead of "life history" (Peacock and Holland 1993; Miller 2000). It takes a sociological perspective on narrated life stories, because life stories are considered to be based on social knowledge here, as related to general social structures. They are narratives that are location-dependent; they take on a certain perspective and occur at a certain point in time. I consider the biographical narratives in these interviews of former industrial workers as expressions of their social positions in hierarchical social space (Bourdieu 1984) today, at the time when the stories were told. Life story interviews have a situational nature since the interviewees narrate how they make sense of their life at a particular moment and from a specific identity-related perspective. The interviewees use a narrative of the past to interpret their lives in the present within a wider social and spatial context.

Biographical narratives allow us – and this makes them so precious for a sociological research project – to conceive of the individual experiences, interpretations and constructions of meaning within their structural context. Based on the understanding that a single case can be indicative of general action structures and interpretation patterns (Bude 1984; Rosenthal 2004), processes of social inequality in biographical narratives can be identified as supraindividual processes, and I perceive them as such. The figuration approach (Elias 1984) helps to grasp the individual narratives especially in their social embeddedness, whereas the "structures of feeling" approach (Williams 1977) focusses particularly on their local contextualisation.

Biographical narratives are also a "self-interpretation" (Ricoeur 1991: 198) and they are reconstructive, because in the narrative the life story is created in an active and dynamic process (Misztal 2003; Olick 2008: 159). Narrated life stories are based on individual memories, but they are not just related to the individual. Rather, individual memories are embedded in publicly circulating narratives that are particular for a certain era of history and for spatial contexts (Lawler 2008: 38). Consequently, memories depend on a certain era, as Karl Mannheim describes it, on a generation "with a common location in the historical dimension of the social process" (Mannheim 1952 [1923]: 290). Raymond Williams also points out that the "structures of feeling" have a chronological and generational dimension, because "no generation speaks quite the same language as its predecessors" (Williams 1977: 131).

The narrated biographical memories belong to a specific social context so that individual memories can be conceived as "collective memories" (Halbwachs 1980 [1950]) having a complex relationship to one another. Narratives are knowledge and as such they are correctly situated in sociology (Alexander 2003). This book refers to a long tradition in social sciences that refers to a social perspective on social knowledge (Berger and Luckmann 1966) and conceptualises personal memory as a social phenomenon such as collective memory, cultural memory or social memory (Nora 1989; Halbwachs 1992 [1941]; Zerubavel 1996; Zerubavel, 2003).[5] Despite further differences between these concepts of memory (Olick and Robbins 1998; Erll and Nünning 2008), it is important to note for the purpose of this book that memory and knowledge are collective matters; they need a social framework and they are transient (Zelizer 1995).

The personal perspective on one's life and on the places where life took place is not an independent perspective of one individual. Biographic memories relate to a common knowledge and to powerful narratives as prevalent in official representations and general discourse. The individual memories are always related to the social, economic, spatial and cultural contexts in which the individual is situated. Through collective memories of a past, individual recollections become memories creating a sense of identity, which then leads to social positionings. Not only does this manifest itself in the personal interviews and in the industrial workers' repetitive nostalgic narratives of an earlier solidary and harmonious community, but also in the focus group interviews. In these groups three to five persons were interviewed, all of whom presented common narratives on shared experiences and knowledge bases during their communicative interactions (Morgan 1996; Przyborski and Wohlrab-Sahr 2010: 101–107). In both interview situations, the individual biographical interviews and the focus group interview, narratives are generated which consist of collective memories shared with one another. As becomes repeatedly evident in the narratives and contextualisations therein of individual experiences as joint experiences of the group of industrial workers, these memories enable individuals to become members of an imagined community (Mills 2010: 14), namely, the community of industrial workers. Maurice Halbwachs' view on the relationship between individual and collective memory is relevant in helping to understand individual biographical narratives in their social embeddedness. He states:

> While the collective memory endures and draws strength from its base in a coherent body of people, it is individuals as group members who remember. While these remembrances are mutually supportive of each other and common to all, individual members still vary in the intensity with which they experience them. I would readily acknowledge that each memory is a viewpoint on the collective memory, that this viewpoint changes as may relationship to other milieus change.
>
> (Halbwachs 1980 [1950]: 48)

Halbwachs views the individual memory as one that is formed by social interactions and communication, and as being closely related to collective memory schemes, thus also being socially shaped. From this perspective, the biographical narratives of the interviewed industrial workers can only be grasped when they are viewed in their social embeddedness, i.e. not as individual but as social memories. This perspective helps in understanding the workers' individual biographical narratives as social and knowledge-based. Collective memories and cultures of memory (Erll 2011) are dynamic and changing. In fact, the framework within which individuals memorise, tell their life stories and socially position themselves is knowledge-related. Mannheim points out that this knowledge has a temporal dimension, which he calls the concept of generation. The membership in such a generation, which Mannheim refers to as a community of destiny, is the result of growing up in the same historical and cultural context. The "big" transformations of socioeconomic and spatial structures are therefore also reflected in individual lives and narrative memories. However – and this is often forgotten with regard to Mannheim – it is not just the belonging to a generation that is knowledge-relevant in a specific way, but for Mannheim it is also the belonging to a class (see also Halbwachs 1980 [1950]: 84), as becomes evident in the following quotation:

> The fact of belonging to the same class, and that of belonging to the same generation or age group, have this in common, that both endow the individuals sharing them with a common location in the social and historical process, and thereby limit them to a specific range of potential experience, predisposing them for a certain characteristic mode of thought and experience, and a characteristic type of historically relevant action.
>
> (Mannheim 1952 [1923]: 291)

Mannheim puts a different emphasis on the relationship between class and knowledge as Marx, who distinguishes between a "class in itself" resulting from the position of having a common relation to the means of production, and a "class for itself," the members being conscious of their class position (Marx 1847). Thus, at least one other factor must be considered in the relationship between class and knowledge: the temporal era reflected in generational knowledge which is formative for collective memories, but also the localities where the narrative memories of the experiences and everyday practices originated are significant, as I will show in the following section.

Transformations: industrial landscapes and the "structures of feeling"

Transformations become evident when post-industrial landscapes resulting from deindustrialisation are encountered, where newly erected office buildings or shopping centres invoke the past industrial sites, be it that the architecture of old structures is visibly integrated (Zukin 1982) or that the name of the previous factory reappears in the name of the new building. Industrial ruins or scrap metal discarded on abandoned sites are also clear testimonials of transformations through which previously functional structures became useless and were abandoned (Edensor 2005b; High and Lewis 2007; Mah 2012; Storm 2014). Another possibility is that they have received a new touristic function (Urry and Larsen 2011: 135–154) as an industrial heritage (Barthel 1996; Hospers 2002; Mieg and Oevermann 2014) or were – upon the initiative of former workers – preserved as "heritage from below" (Robertson 2008) to be a testimonial of the workers' own history.

Sharon Zukin understands landscapes as a social product, as an "ensemble of material and social practices and their symbolic representations" (Zukin 1993: 16). Landscapes may be read as texts, and as such they are not innocent elements, but materialised, powerful discourses reproducing certain meanings and also functioning as identity-establishing elements. Looking upon landscapes, we discover more than just materiality, because we also perceive representations charged with social and political processes, and which are an element of the "structures of feeling." Since the dawn of the age of industrialisation, industrial landscapes with their sprawling factories, smokestacks or headframes have been symbols of modernity and progress. In early capitalism, they were marks of an ambivalent progress with enormous social problems and conflicts, as they were exemplarily described by Friedrich Engels (Engels 1845). Later, in the course of the Taylorist approach of management with the development of its unique division of labour and assembly line work, the industrial landscapes and their products became – like the Ford Model T – a symbol of Fordism. This epoch had been characterised by a cooperative social partnership, a rise in the general wage share, the development of labour rights, the expansion of the welfare state and the increased possibility of general consumption. Yet in the old industrial centres of North America and Europe, industrial landscapes have changed. Factories were closed, demolished and transformed into offices or lofts, former workers' housing estates were sold or privatised, work processes were rationalised and physical labour relocated or replaced.

Changed former industrial areas are an excellent example of spaces representing general socioeconomic transformations. Their altered spatial form can be taken as an example of the spatial relocation of industrial work processes in an increasingly international division of labour (Fröbel, Heinrichs and Kreye 1980). Later this was understood as economic globalisation (Giddens 1990; Beck 1999; Castells 2010) and as transitions from an "industrial" to a "post-industrial" society (Bell 1974), from "Fordism" to "post-Fordism" (Lipietz 1992; Jessop 1995) or from "modernity" to "post-modernity" (Harvey 1990; Jameson 1992).

Yet the process of industrial transition at a local level has occurred in different forms. The radical change in Detroit, manifested in industrial fallow land (Millington 2013), or the shut-down of the mines in South Yorkshire (Kirk 2012), has a different quality compared to the industrial transformation in Nuremberg, where, aside from the demolition of industrial structures, transformation has also resulted in redesigned and newly erected factory buildings. By no means has industrial work vanished in Germany; after all, the manufacturing sector employs also 10.6 million employees (24.1% of total workforce) in 2017 (Statistisches Bundesamt 2018: 359ff.).[6]

Even far away from the work places, in the residential areas or public spaces, transformations are generally visible as evidence of the past, such as in monuments or memorial plaques reminding us of former founders of factories or housing estates, and whose names are also seen on street signs. However, transformations may not necessarily be apparent for everybody. Those familiar with the area from their own experience or by having adopted stories from others may see much more than newcomers to the region, who are not able to associate the high-rise office building and the shopping centre, built on former factory sites, with their own memories of the area. The newcomers are incapable of reading from the left-over traces of the past the signs pointing to what is now absent.

In addition to generational knowledge, i.e. knowledge related to class and other dimensions of social identities, such as gender or "ethnicity," it is the local context which represents a source of specific knowledge. In that sense, the figure of the stranger by Alfred Schütz is foreign in the new environment, because a stranger who has migrated to a new location brings along acquired knowledge, which no longer matches the new environment and must be learnt anew (Schütz 1944).

Memories are often bound to landscapes and places (Casey 1987; Hayden 1995; Nora 1996; Mills 2010; Jones and Garde-Hansen 2012). This is not just the case with national memorial sites, the "lieux de mémoire" (Nora 1989),[7] such as museums, poetry or monuments, which (are meant to) produce narratives of national identity, and which – as sites of collective memory – contribute to the building of nations as imagined communities (Anderson 1983). Halbwachs puts it as follows: "every collective memory unfolds within a spatial framework" (Halbwachs 1980 [1950]: 140). However, individual biographical memories are also frequently bound to places, especially to those of one's own childhood (Tuan 1977; Jones 2005), where one lived and worked (Wheeler 2014) or to places where traumatic experiences occurred (Trigg 2009; Morrissey 2012). Karen Till also recommends carrying out memory studies investigating the individuals' and social groups' pasts by focussing on their ties to certain places, because: "places become a part of us, even when held in common, through the intimate relationships individuals and groups have with them" (Till 2008: 108).

As Tim Edensor (2008) demonstrates in his study of transformed landscapes of the working class in Manchester, these places that have undergone remarkable change still contain traces of past materiality, former cultural and social practices, and certain modes of thinking or forms of experiences. These traces, which may still be detected locally today, may trigger memories in those individuals who have lived or gained experiences there. This may occur through a direct bodily encounter on location, as I experienced in joint field inspections with interview partners, or in relived encounters in the interview situation. Such traces have a double character: they are the visible or felt remains of a past time, while also revealing that something is absent today (Meier, Frers and Sigvardsdotter 2013). Encountering such traces awakens memories of a previous life (Wheeler 2014) so that the individual trace in the narrated memory becomes a part of a whole: "the power of synecdoche in landscapes is that such a fragment takes on greater meaning: the projected meaning of the imagined whole" (DeLyser 2001). The encounters with such traces pointing to something absent are often experienced by the interviewees as a loss of something past in regard to today's situation. Only with the experience of a past is it possible for something to appear absent today (Frers 2013).

The memories of that which is absent today are also social positionings with which one's own position in the social structure can be reflected as part of its transition. In retrospect, the narrators' present-day memories of common experiences in an idealised and harmoniously viewed society represent relevant social self-positionings, thereby revealing information on today's changed social position. In the memories stimulated by confronting the traces of the past, such as the ruins of the former workplace, the past becomes visible. As expressed by the metaphor of the haunting ghost, the damages suffered and experiences of loss are shocking, because these are not just individually narrated memories, but also social memories in that they are related to the early work and housing experiences of members of a certain class. Thus, they are specific memories, since they are based on specific knowledge and experiences, because:

> haunting is a very particular way of knowing what has happened or is happening. Being haunted draws us affectively, sometimes against our will and always a bit magically, into the structure of feeling of a reality we come to experience, not as cold knowledge, but as a transformative recognition.
>
> (Gordon 2008: 8)

Today's encounter with the haunting ghost simultaneously shows both the memories of a nostalgically idealised, golden past and today's experience of the loss of this past. Nostalgia is the painful (algos) sentimentality for returning home (nóstos). The word was coined by Swiss doctor Johannes Hofer in 1688 to describe the anxieties displayed by Swiss mercenaries. It is the current idealisation of the past; a "memory with the pain removed. The pain is today" (Lowenthal 1985: 8). Nostalgia is a home that no longer exists and has never existed in the idealised way it is memorised (Boym 2001; Duyvendak 2011). Such a nostalgic view on behalf of industrial workers (while simultaneously blocking out earlier social exclusions, problems and conflicts) in changed industrial landscapes or former working-class housing areas has been covered in various studies – particularly in Great Britain (Charlesworth 2000; Kirk 2007; Rogaly and Taylor 2009; Blackshaw 2013). Strangleman (2014) justifiably points out that due to the term "nostalgia" a more extensive social science analysis is being suppressed, because "the term 'nostalgia' is used as a card to crudely trump what is often more insightful analysis" (Strangleman 2014). Therefore, I propose in this book, following a critical review of nostalgia in narrated memories, to analyse nostalgia in these memories as a cultural practice (Wheeler 2017) that "depends on where the speaker stands in the landscape of the present" (Stewart 1988: 227). In this context, class also becomes relevant through the emotions expressed in the narratives, such as mourning and anger in conjunction with the loss of acknowledgement of physical labour (see Chapter 4), experiencing helplessness to act when faced with the demolition of one's former workplace (see Chapter 5) or one's own social decline within an established-outsider figuration (see Chapter 7).

The nostalgic narratives of past harmonically idealised community life in the residential neighbourhood, as I detail it in Chapter 7, are therefore to be understood as present social positionings on behalf of the long-established residents (Blokland 2003). They are a manifestation of drawing a line vis-à-vis the newcomers, because it is always "a group of 'us' who remember, as opposed to the recently arrived who can't because they weren't there. This kind of 'boundary work' creates divisions between 'insiders' and 'outsiders'" (Savage 2014: 32). Again and again, the insiders look back to a former social community that in their narratives is constructed as location-based and socially homogenous. Even if "community studies" do have the potential to make social transformations at a defined local level comprehensible (Mah 2012: 4), former studies on the community in working-class areas (such as Young and Willmott 1957; Dennis et al. 1956) can be justifiably criticised in that these tend to overemphasise social solidarity and homogeneity within the community, thereby blotting out former conflicts as well as social diversity (Blackshaw 2010: 62–63). Similar to these studies, the interviewees nostalgic view is also influenced by such assessments. Blotting out conflicts and social diversity in the past occurs (as I will elaborate later more in detail on the established-outsider figuration) in association with the change in the interviewees' social positions, and is therefore also related to the question as to who has the power to define the social rules in the local community and to enforce them by setting the standards (see Chapters 7 and 8).

> In general, we may say that whenever a person (young or old) feels that the world is changing too rapidly, his [sic] characteristic response is to evoke an idealised and stable past. On the other hand, when a person feels that he himself is directing the change and in control of affairs of importance to him, then nostalgia has no place in his life: action rather than mementos of the past will support his sense of identity.
>
> (Tuan 1977: 188)

Like the nostalgic look into the past, narrative memories occur in a larger socioeconomic and also local context (as elaborated in Chapter 2). At the same time, these are memories of specific social groups whose social positions have changed, as has been the case with industrial workers. Memories reveal information about these social positions here and now and, in that sense, are suitable for studying social inequality.

As already mentioned above, the "structures of feeling" approach by Raymond Williams lends itself to the understanding of narrative memories in a broader context. This approach is based on understanding culture as an everyday culture, as "a whole way of life" (Williams 1979). Everyday cultural practices are manifested in, for example, actions, meanings, texts or things, i.e. an expression of a specific way of life. The concept of the "structures of feeling" thereby indicates a structure overarching the individual elements, mediating between the individual and the social.

The thesis is that a social formation may be best described by interrelated routines and the social practices characterising them. It is a structure which is felt and experienced and which accompanies specific economic and political structures. It includes:

> characteristic elements of impulse, restraint, and tone; specifically affective elements of consciousness and relationship: not feeling against thought, but thought as felt and feeling as thought: practical consciousness of a present kind, in a living and interrelating continuity. We are then defining these elements as a 'structure': as a set, with specific internal relations, a tone interlocking and in tension.
>
> (Williams 1977: 132)

Williams also views his concept as an analysis perspective for nation states (in his studies on the examples of England and Wales); in addition, it can also be used for analyses of regions and cities (Taylor, Evans and Fraser 1996; Löw 2008; Kirk, Contrepois and Jefferys 2012). "Structures of feeling" manifest themselves in the fine arts, literature and generally also in representations of places and landscapes, and even in the self-descriptions of social communities. They are "meanings and values as they are actually lived and felt" (Williams 1977: 132). With this perspective we are able to link social structures – such as social inequalities – with individual narratives as well as with the analysis of semantic figures in texts and official representations. Together with the differentiation between "dominant," "residual" and "emergent" proposed by Williams, this opens a perspective on social practices and experiences, which is more than merely a view on individual experiences of structures of social inequality. It is a view that emphasises transformations and also makes the case for acknowledging the past ("residual") and the future ("emergent") when considering the current "structures of feeling."

Even if the "structures of feeling" are characteristic for a generation, Williams' concept shows much more clearly than Mannheim's sociology of knowledge generation-concept that transformations do not occur seamlessly and totally, but that the past is an "effective element of the present" (Williams 1977: 122), as elaborated above with the examples of absence and the ghost metaphor. Thus, at the same time "new meanings and values, new practices, new relationships and kinds of relationships" are constantly created in the present (Williams 1977: 123).

This perspective allows us to understand current practices and emotions analysed in the following chapters of this book in consideration of their past and the signs of their future, while also drawing a connexion to the analysis of the dominant discourse and counter-discourse as well as discursive practices and practices of resistance (de Certeau 1988) as dynamic and interrelated with one another (elaborated in Chapter 6). The cultural science focus in Williams' approach is based on understanding emotions as "a cluster of emotions" (Hunt 2012: 138), which are characteristic for a particular era and are found in cultural artefacts. I perceive this grasp of emotions in a certain time and society as a contribution to the analysis of a social structure, since Williams' approach allows a perspective in which processes of social inequality are represented by means of individual narratives. Consequently, class can also be understood as emotion. These emotions are no longer seen as being personal, coincidental or unique, but rather as common feelings of classes and social groups within the social structure.

Norbert Elias chooses yet another originally sociological emphasis, an approach with which emotions of individual social groups may be examined and understood as an expression of their social positions in a fabric of social inequality. Elias' figuration approach offers a more analytical view on the relationship between social groups and their changes, something that complements Williams' perspective. With a much more clear focus in comparison to the "structures of feeling" approach, the figuration approach allows an analysis of social inequality as a processual power inequality between social groups, at the same time also considering the constitution of self and others. This makes it possible to analyse the individuals' emotions in connexion with their social position and the changes thereof.

Transformations: social position and figuration

This book shows that individual narratives, identity positionings and social interactions are related to the general processes of social and spatial interactions. It was particularly Norbert Elias and his research on the change of figurations that shaped this understanding of a sociology that conceptualises the society and the individual as closely and processually linked (Baur and Ernst 2011; Baur 2016). Elias developed:

> a picture of people who, through their basic dispositions and inclinations, are directed towards and linked with each other in the most diverse ways. These people make up webs of interdependence or figurations of many kinds, characterized by power balances of many sorts, such as families, schools, towns, social strata, or states.
>
> (Elias 1984: 15)

His basic idea is to remove the conceptual separation of the individual and the society and instead conceive of individuals in their plurality and interrelatedness with one another.[8] The figuration concept illustrates these networks of relationships and reciprocal interdependencies among the individuals. Figurations cannot be explained independent of individuals, just as individuals do not exist independent of figurations (Elias and Scotson 1965). Figurations may consist of either small and manageable groups, such as a bridge club or a kindergarten group, or larger networks with more differentiated interdependence, such as a nation, a city or a neighbourhood. Hence, figurations are space-building processes (Löw 2016) that may also be characterised by their specific space. Similar to Erving Goffman, Elias studies social actions at the interaction level, yet emphasises in his analysis of power processes with his figuration concept (Willems 1997) more strongly in comparison to Goffman's frame analysis (1977), thereby showing that power is an attribute of relationships and is best applied in connexion with the reference to more or less fluctuating power changes (Elias 1984).

For Elias, power is a concept based on relationships with which a balance of tension is expressed in a figuration. This power balance is not static but changes over time. This understanding of dynamic and interdependent power structures manifested in figurations is helpful in order to analyse social transformations, such as in the case example of South Nuremberg[9] in this book. Elias and Scotson studied such a figuration in the suburb of Winston Parva.[10] In this case they demonstrated that there had been a power and status difference between old-established and newly arrived workers, the established and the outsiders, at the spatial level (Elias and Scotson speak of three different zones).[11] This clearly shows that the old-established families actively kept the newly arrived families at a distance, thereby securing their own status (see also Barwick 2017). This is to say, their relative power within the established-outsider figuration was especially fed by stable and strong social networks within the group of the established, whereas the newcomers only kept weakly developed networks among themselves, not yet having established their own group identity.

Figurations are processual, and along with the changing industrial areas, there is also a change taking place in the local figuration and the social positions within such a figuration. These are transformations that are accompanied by changing social inequality structures, leading to newly formed social power relations. In their study Elias and Scotson show how an established-outsider relationship develops; I will outline in Chapters 7 and 8 that such a figuration is dynamic and that the power structure within the established-outsider figuration may change or even reverse. The dynamic of the figuration becomes evident in the narrative, since the interviewees correlate today's situation with that of past times. Thus they offer a personal perspective on a figuration relationship that expresses their social position in this inequality fabric, defining thereby the self and the other. In this sense, individual biographical narratives represent individuals' self-positionings that do not just reveal the individuals' changed social identity. Instead, these social positionings are understood as a narrative of a change in social positioning within a social structure in a transformed environment.

Transformations: class and work

> The unquestioning way in which the term "individual" is used in conversation in the more developed societies of our day that the differences between people, their I-identity, are valued more highly than what they have in common, their we-identity.
>
> (Elias 2001: 156)

It is not to be necessarily taken for granted today that a social scientist concentrates on the work and social role of a person in the working class. In fact, the challenges of years of intensive, physical gainful employment, the workers' social structural positions within a changed society as well as their affiliation to those with similar empirical knowledge had initially not been a focus – or at least no longer a focus, to be exact. Well into the 1970s, social science studies on workers (and rarely on female workers) were popular in Germany. The main area of interest at the time lay particularly on identifying the workers' class consciousness (Deppe 1971; Kudera, Ruff and Schmidt 1982), the existence of which in the beginning had been cautiously (Popitz et al. 1957), later on more distinctly (Kern and Schumann 1970)[12] questioned, while showing workers' internal social differentiation (such as between unskilled and skilled workers) (Schumann 1999).

Almost at the same time, as a consequence of economic growth, further development of welfare state security, the general gains in spending power and a general upward mobility (Beck 1992), it was assumed that a dissolution of the proletarian milieu (Mooser 1984) and a loss in the relevance of class and social strata in life would occur (Beck 1992). This thesis of a "death of class" (Pakulski and Waters 1996) was placed in context to general individualisation processes within a "reflexive modernity" (Giddens 1994; Beck 2007). Behind this thesis is the assumption that individuals were released from traditional ties, and roles (such as class and strata, but also gender, neighbourhood or family, see also Beck and Beck-Gernsheim 2002) and that along with this, traditional securities had been lost and individuals would have now greater choices, which, of course, they would have to reflexively use for their "bricolage existence" (Hitzler and Honer 1994; Hitzler 2003) in the "multi-option society" (Gross and Bertschi 2006). For Beck this led to social classes having become "zombie-categories," to "living dead categories, which blind the social sciences to the rapidly changing realities inside the nation-state containers and outside as well" (Beck 2002: 24). Thus, for a time the concept of class had almost disappeared. With the "cultural turn," attention was paid to other – often previously neglected – categories of social inequality. What previously may have been criticised in many studies on the working class, namely that other categories of social inequality (gender and "ethnicity") were ignored, was now reversed – this time by largely blotting out class. Bell hooks came up with the following statement:

> Nowadays it is fashionable to talk about race and gender; the uncool subject is class.
>
> (hooks 2000: VII)

Some time after the end of the short period of seemingly everlasting prosperity (Lutz 1989) in the "golden age of capitalism" (Hobsbawm 1998: 324–501; Lipietz 1998), the scientific discourse in the late 1980s and especially in the 1990s was dominated by the assessment that – due to the change of work towards more flexible and insecure forms of employment – work in general had lost its identity-forming meaning (Rifkin 1995; Beck 2000; Bauman 2005) or, in terms of a future utopia marked by the optimism of progress, should lose it (Gorz 1999). This, in turn, had led to a "corrosion of character" (Sennett 1998). The thesis was that this had all led to a replacement of a work-based society by a consumption-based society (Featherstone 1991; Ransome 2005). Hence, the previously assumed close relationship between work and identity had been frequently replaced by a connexion between consumption practices and identity (Bauman 2007), something that has been applied, for example, in Asia or South America to characterise a new class, the "new middle classes" (Robison and Goodman 1996; Lange and Meier 2009; Elfick 2011; Yuk-Ha Tsang 2014). This assumed loss of relevance as a major identity-forming element and the thesis of the dissolution of class derived thereof was often criticised and in many empirical studies falsified (Strangleman 2007; Atkinson 2010; Kirk and Wall 2011; Strangleman 2012). It became clear that "work remains an importance source of identity, meaning and social affiliation" (Doherty 2009).

Today the emphasis of empirical studies in German sociology lies on the relevance of class or strata for two groups in particular. First, there is the precariously employed "lower social strata" that is especially jeopardised in its social participation, which once again shifts the focus (Altenhain et al. 2008; Chassé 2010; Dörre et al. 2013) to the return of the social question (Bude and Willisch 2007; Kronauer 2010). Second, as a result of the transition to more flexible types of work, there is the more highly qualified middle class, such as the "creative class" (Florida 2004), or the highly mobile "migrant professionals" (Meier 2015) employed in the service sector, who as "self-entrepreneurial workforce" (Pongratz and Voss 2003) or as an "entrepreneurial self" (Bröckling 2016) experience a subjectification of work (Lohr and Nickel 2009). Unlike in the research on the lower social strata, the reference to class or strata in the research on the qualified middle class has been, if at all, established only implicitly. However, industrial workers, and therefore the traditional working class, have largely disappeared in the research on social inequality in Germany.[13] The fact that sociology has turned away from the inequality category of class, thereby also from the working class, has not only limited the research on social inequality and its definition, but also created further gaps, because:

> How workers – who formally represent about 28% of all those gainfully employed after all – think about their co-workers, their companies, their lives beyond employment today – is despite existing public opinion surveys – largely unknown. The same applies for employees in a broader sense.
>
> (Dörre, Happ and Matuschek 2013: 23)
> (translation by Lars Meier)

Since 2005 and the standardisation of the pension insurance plans, labour, social and collective bargaining laws no longer make a difference between employees and workers in Germany (Meine 2005). The term "worker" specifically refers to physical gainful employment, frequently under harmful environmental influences in which workers are exposed to above-average health risks and, compared to employees and civil servants, receive on average a lower income (Geißler 2011: 191f.).

Without a doubt, work has changed; precarious forms of employment as well as temporary appointment, part-time and mini-jobs have increased. Boltanski and Chiapello (2003) indicate that a new form of capitalism has developed, which manifests itself in the rising challenges at work with regard to more expected flexibility and in creating a project-based polis.[14] Robert Castel mentions that work today has lost a role which it embodied during the era of the industrial society, namely the role of a social integrator, particularly for the "low social classes." His argument is that work has become more precarious and that nowadays a part of the formerly integrated working class as well as the lower middle class are threatened by a downfall. Castel calls this the "destabilization of the stable" concluding that paid work has lost its social integration function (Castel 2000: 357),[15] resulting in a return of social insecurity (Castel 2009). At the same time, the change of work is correlated with the change in social structure. An increasing precariousness of work, for example, will generate a clear rise in the relative poverty quote (see also footnote 1), thus a "return of poverty" (Honneth 1993), a shrinking of the middle class (Grabka and Frick 2008; Vogel 2010) and a general increase in social inequality (Groh-Samberg 2004, 2008), which also explains the massive rise in assets of the wealthy (Goebel, Grabka and Schröder 2015). Instead of a general trickledown effect (Beck 1992) one should rather speak of a "paternoster lift effect"; the rise of some social classes goes hand in hand with the decline of another (Butterwegge 2006).

The diagnosed increase in precariousness and poverty led to a refertilisation of the social structural concept of class (Groh-Samberg 2008; for an overview on literature see Kraemer 2014), and not only in German sociology. In the media as well, a reorientation towards the concept of class appeared that had long been scorned. However, the concept of class became henceforth a stigmatising designation, termed "lower social strata" or "underclass," since class was associated with the attribution of features of the "underserving poor" (Castel 2000), i.e. a group of underprivileged individuals who are made responsible for their own situation of poverty (unlike the "deserving poor"). From this perspective, poverty is not justified socially or economically, but rather via cultural practices, i.e. a "culture of poverty" (Lewis 1966). Several studies demonstrate that such a perspective is adopted in media and political discourses, for instance, in England (Gidley and Rooke 2010; Jones 2011) or Germany (Fohrbeck, Hirseland and Ramos Lobato 2014), in order to brand the terms "low social class" and "low social strata" in a discriminatory fashion, resulting in a stereotypical attribution of negatively assessed cultural features and practices. The identity-forming impact of such a "speech act" was evidenced by Judith Butler using the example of gender identities. "Within speech act theory, a performative is that discursive practice that enacts or produces that which it names" (Butler 1993: 13).

Such a potent and discriminatory attribution of cultural features was rightfully criticised as classism (Adams et al. 2000: Section 7), or was criticised in the research on "ethnicity" as "groupism," which resulted in a demand for "ethnicity without groups" (Brubaker 2006). Undoubtedly, the concept of class has posed problems and challenges for the social structure analysis, in that the categories of class (or strata, or milieu) are "nominal entities far from being what might be referred to as real existing groups," and as a result these designated groups vary depending on the definition. Inevitably the question arises at the empirical level as to "who belongs where and why?" (Berking 2010: 65).

Proposing a different path, this book uses class not as a powerful attribution of certain features, but as an analytical category for capturing processes of social inequality. Not only does the concept of class reveal processes of social inequality and social struggles – in the terms of a culture as "a whole way of struggle" (Thompson 1963) – it also gives them a designation. Tackling the challenge of rendering class as an analytical category beneficial again has been taken on by the approach of intersectionality.[16] This approach claims to analyse the different social inequality categories, such as class, gender and "ethnicity," in both their intersection and interaction. Even though it was the original intention of this approach to analyse the interactions of the forms of discrimination, this perspective is in principle also suitable for analysing social inequality in general. On the other hand, there is dissent in terms of the differentiating categories (such as body, age, health, etc.) (Winker and Degele 2009; Giebeler, Rademacher and Schulze 2013; Lutz, Herrera Vivar and Supik 2013), which need to be considered in intersectionality, resulting in the selection of differentiating categories appearing at times somewhat random and additive. One of the problems associated with intersectionality analysis is that the specific logic of the different social inequality categories are not adequately respected and that, for instance, "ethnicity" cannot be treated in the same fashion as class (Skeggs in Phoenix 2006; Yuval-Davis 2006; Žižek 2012: 33). Even if the intersectionality analysis accepts class as a crucial inequality category, the approach was criticised for the fact that class frequently receives inadequate and poorly elaborated consideration (Kofman 2008; Garske 2013), which therefore results in the fact that "class is sometimes the unstated absent presence" (Woodward et al. 2014: 427).

What is class?

Class is a relational category of social inequality and is only conceivable when compared to other classes (Thompson 1963). Class also has a dynamic character and constitutes itself through "material and symbolic struggles," which is why an analysis of class should have the goal "to capture the ambiguity produced through struggle and fuzzy boundaries, rather than to fix it in place in order to measure and know it" (Skeggs 2004: 5). Pierre Bourdieu shows that class may also be understood in terms of social practices and is reproduced by such everyday practices (Bourdieu 1984; Bourdieu 1990). Debating the concept of habitus, Andrew Sayer argues that emotions are a neglected aspect in Bourdieu's work, while they are in fact of major relevance for the experience of class. He elaborates that:

> class matters to us not only because of differences in material wealth and economic security, but also because it affects our access to things, relationships, experiences and practices (…). At the same time it affects how others value us and respond to us, which in turn affects our sense of self-worth. We are evaluative beings, continually monitoring and assessing our behaviour and that of others, needing their approval and respect (…). Condescension, deference, shame, guilt, envy, resentment, arrogance, contempt, fear and mistrust, or simply incomprehension and avoidance, typify relations between people of different classes.
>
> (Sayer 2005: 1)

Following this perspective, my book analyses class as a contested social position (as "a whole way of struggle," Thompson 1963), manifesting itself in everyday practices (Adams and Raisborough 2008; Le Roux et al. 2008), being dynamic, functioning as a source of identification for a social group (definition of self and other) (Reid 1998; Skeggs 2004), having emotional efficacy (Reay 2005; Sayer 2005; Kirk 2007), and thereby also finding a specific expression in joint narrative memories (Meier and Aytekin 2019). The concept of class thus indicates more than just an unequal distribution of different resources or different types of capital (Bourdieu 1984), as various studies claim. Therefore, with the understanding presented here, my book has a different focus than these empirical studies, which, either in line with Weber, define class in terms of the employees' work relationships or market situations (Erikson and Goldthorpe 1992; Goldthorpe 1996) or, referring to Marx, define class along the line of relationships of exploitation and capital property (Wright 1997). Depending on the parameters selected, these other studies indicate conflicting data regarding the number of classes and class differentiations.

However, I will show that the affiliation to the working class also becomes relevant in regard to joint emotions, such as anger or mourning, occurring as a consequence of experiencing a devaluation of physical labour as part of the worker habitus (Charlesworth 2000) or due to one's own lack of influence. This also explains the specific nostalgic narrative perspective: this is a nostalgia that doesn't exactly look back on times of prosperity. In fact, on the surface, the nostalgic perspective conflicts with the actual prosperity gain and the industrial workers' rise; on the other hand, it does not conflict with workers' changed and emotionally perceptible social position in a changed industrial area with a transformed established-outsider figuration and structure of recognition (Honneth 1996).

Outline

This book consists of nine chapters, in which the consequences of social and spatial transformations of industrial landscapes are analysed – for the individuals living there and as to how they cope on a day-to-day basis with the changes of their social positions in a transformed local social structure. Hereby, the relevance of class as a dynamic and contested social position, which has also an emotional effect, is an important emphasis. The individual chapters are divided into three major sections.

In the first section the social and spatial change in the industrial transformation region of South Nuremberg is presented against the backdrop of a general socioeconomic change. This section provides information about the context necessary for a better understanding of the following sections.

Chapter 2 introduces the field methods and specifically focusses on the biographical interviews in Nuremberg. Based on an overview of the socioeconomic development of Germany after 1945, the chapter describes the context in which Nuremberg's specific history and the interviewees' narratives can be understood. It becomes apparent that Nuremberg's transformation always involved social change, from the beginning of industrialisation of the "red" working-class city, its prominent role during the Nazi era and through to the incipient deindustrialisation accompanied by a strengthening of the service sector. The thesis underlying this chapter implies that the city had attained a specific imprint due to the importance of its industry. This imprint has a relevance for the social identities of the persons living and working there as a "structure of feeling" (Williams 1977) and – according to the concept of Raymond Williams – can be taken as a "local structure of feeling" (Taylor, Evans and Fraser 1996) or as an "inherent logic" (Berking and Löw 2008; Löw 2008; for an overview of the discussion see Frank et al. 2013).

The described socioeconomic transformations go hand in hand with the changes in these "structures of feeling" and the social identities. This chapter provides the context in which the workers' coping strategies in terms of the changes in their social positions in a transformed local social structure need to be understood in the later chapters.

Chapter 3 presents a summary of the transformation of class and gender based on a secondary analysis of statistical data and on a field survey that I performed in Nuremberg. This also reveals the change in social structure. The chapter points to dimensions in which class became relevant in the conducted interviews: as an expression of specific individual interests, in feelings of powerlessness due to one's social position, in the attribution of specific everyday cultural practices regarding the self and the other, and as a description of unequal disposition of economic resources. The change and consistency of gender in South Nuremberg will be analysed based on two case examples: men's domestic work and women's industrial production work.

The second section of the book contains three chapters focussing on senses of place and on what is absent today, but is present in the interviews in terms of their relevance for today's social positionings. For Williams, the local "structure of feeling" is also manifested in the representations of a specific space, such as in fine arts, literature or in media texts and political discourses. Such visual images and language function together as "systems of representation" (Hall 1997) or, as Williams puts it, as "official consciousness" (1977: 130).

In Chapter 4 such a "system of representation" is analysed based on the official representations of South Nuremberg in its transformation. In his approach, Williams shows that the "structures of feeling" also have a processual character. It implies that Nuremberg's representation as a working-class city with individuals involved in physical labour changed to a representation of the city as a service centre. People engaged in physical labour no longer fit into this image of an academic service city that endeavoured to present an attractive image for the "creative class" – as Richard Florida (2004) puts it. For the former workers this change led to a devaluation of their skills and working knowledge, which had allowed them to use their bodies for a formerly recognised labour. In their narratives these former workers are therefore always eager to justify their skills as valuable and useful and to demonstrate their abilities (renovation and handicraft work at home), thereby justifying their efforts and their adjustments to the newly recognised forms of knowledge (via advanced training). The chapter makes it clear that transformations, such as from a working-class city to a service city, find their expressions in biographic narratives and self-concepts. It also becomes evident that workers do not only passively endure, but rather shape these changes by participating in advanced training and making an effort to attain this newly recognised knowledge. On the other hand, they lament emotionally and along class lines (Sayer 2005) the loss of public recognition of their skills as industrial workers and emphasise time and again the practical relevance of their own knowledge at home, comparing it with the knowledge that is recognised today. In the analysis of the contrast between an official representation, which optimistically describes the transformation as a chance for prosperity, and the nostalgic narratives of the workers, in which the change is accompanied by negative emotions, the chapter makes clear the relevance of class for the workers' emotional memories, their nostalgic view and therefore also their current positioning in the transformed south of Nuremberg.

Chapter 5 is dedicated to the experiences in which former industrial workers visit their old workplaces, even if these no longer exist except as industrial ruins or transformed buildings. This chapter illustrates how the workplace becomes a location wherein the workers develop a close emotional attachment so that it becomes a kind of home for them. This results in workers visiting these places repeatedly (some even almost every day), long after the former factory has been demolished. The encounter with the location brings back memories; for the workers, past occurrences and work routines reappear almost eerily on the premises of the now demolished buildings and redesigned sites. Avery Gordon (2008) argues that the encounter with haunting ghosts is a terrifying experience, because the ghost exposes experiences of past losses, which originated by means of violent events. This sense of loss that former workers have experienced with the loss of their job and the demolition of their factories is made visible with the metaphor of the haunting ghost. Derrida, who introduced this metaphor of the ghost ("spectre"), argues that with this the relationship between the present and the past becomes significant (Derrida 1994). As opposed to the memories referring to a closed process, the metaphor of the ghost indicates that which is not yet closed, has not yet died, and which may suddenly and dreadfully appear during the encounter. The metaphor allows the tie between institution and individual, between a social structure and a personal situation, indeed even between history and biography to be revealed. The ghosts indicate that the objective change is being processed and shaped at the individual level. Today the encounters with these places are emotionally challenging and painful for the former workers. In confrontation with these places memories of better times are brought back, becoming eerily visible. However, such an encounter is also a productive process, not only because it gives the workers the chance to cope with the loss, but also to reassure themselves of their own identity as workers, of their identity as a class with a direct emotional and oftentimes even joint experience. After all, the ghosts are not visible to everyone, but solely to them, the former workers.

Chapter 6 takes a look at a different aspect of the transformation of public space in South Nuremberg, namely, the use of public space for practices of resistance (de Certeau 1988). The nostalgic view of the former public space taken on by the workers in their biographical narratives is seen in connexion with a changed assessment of the practices of resistance in Nuremberg's public space. While these had earlier been understood as the workers' "own" practices with a positive connotation, as they were considered necessary for one's socialisation, these practices today are viewed as belonging to "the others" and are assessed as threatening. It is shown in this chapter that the practices of resistance have a temporal dimension in terms of duration and in a specific historical context in which they occur, but also in terms of the point in time in which they are remembered and told. The nostalgic memory of such practices is also an expression of a changed social positioning on behalf of those who at the time had the privilege to set the rules of resistance. This contrast between the past practices of resistance and those in the present reveals their distinctive dimension: having been valuable practices for one's own socialisation in the past, they now have turned into practices of others "contaminating" the public space (Douglas 1966).

The third section includes two chapters in which community transformations and social encounters are analysed.

In Chapter 7 the transformation of a local community and its social diversity is critically analysed. Along with a change in the hierarchical relationship between the established and the outsiders (Elias and Scotson 1965), we can also see a changed perception and interaction with the "others." Using the case example of the former MAN (Maschinenfabrik Augsburg-Nürnberg Aktiengesellschaft) workers' settlement in Werderau, it is demonstrated that communities are not just created as imagined communities (Anderson 1983) through narratives and myths, but also by means of solid regulations. The power of the established in Werderau was embodied in close-knit social networks and in the rules of the MAN corporation and the housing cooperative. The latter set the cultural practices among the established residents as a quasi-natural standard to which the outsiders had to adapt. In retrospect, the established interpret their power and control over the cultural practices of the outsiders as a life in harmony and solidarity. After the garden city of Werderau was sold and the housing cooperative closed, the organisation that supported the established in their positions and their cultural practices as a standard was also gone. The loss of power of the former established was closely linked to how they coped with their general social decline and the former outsiders' social climb. The established no longer controlled which cultural practices were allowed. The contrast between their memories of former times and their situation today reveals their frustration at the loss of their former powerful position. With their new social role as those who are no longer the established, the nostalgic view of those MAN workers without migration experience regarding their past can also be seen as a longing for their former powerful position in Werderau as well as for their position within the established-outsider hierarchy. The loss of power of the established former workers was closely linked to how they coped with their general social decline and the former outsiders' social ascent.

In Chapter 8 the biographical narrative of Emilio, a former industrial worker and outsider in the district of Werderau, is analysed. Unlike the narratives of the formerly established and well-settled, Emilio's narrative is not defined by a nostalgic view of an idealised and lost home. It becomes clear that his integration into a transnational family network, his biographical and migration-dependent experiences regarding his assimilation into new localities and social structures are today resources for him, enabling him to view Nuremberg's spatial and social transformation without nostalgia – unlike those factory workers who had not migrated to Nuremberg.

Against the backdrop of the book's main findings, theoretical implications and consequences are discussed in the conclusion (Chapter 9).

This book investigates the consequences of social transformations for individuals living in South Nuremberg and their day-to-day coping with the changes of their social positions in a changed social structure. It explains not only the relevance of class as a dynamically contested and emotional social experience, but also how social inequality is individually experienced. It becomes evident that class is more than just a position in the relations of production. Rather, class is also emotionally sensed by the individual. This manifests itself particularly in how the workers cope with the changes regarding their social positions in a transformed figuration, which is conceived of as a "structure of feeling" as part of a certain era. This "structure of feeling (…) operates in the most delicate and least tangible parts of our activity" (Williams 1965: 64). Since the change in the "structures of feeling" – and this brings me back to Walter Benjamin's initial quote – is also accompanied by a change in perception "conditioned not only by nature but by history" (Benjamin (2008 [1936]: 23), there are, of course, methodical consequences for the analysis of social inequality.

The research on social inequality, diversity and class nowadays requires that the present be not handled as an era that is cut off from the future and the past. Instead, as shown by Williams, the present comprises both the "emergent" and the "residual." The goal is to draw the attention to the fact that the individual biographical narratives limited to a certain time are conditioned by history, and to understand them as social memories embedded in generally circulating narratives and knowledge structures specific to certain historical eras and spatial contexts. This renders the nostalgic view back in time and the emotional realisation of absence visible as social positionings in the present. This is how social inequality and class in their dynamic with one another can be conceived of as contested. On the other hand, this dynamic can only be understood in relation to its past. This research perspective also requires identifying the emotional aspect of class and comprehending what is absent, missed and unwanted today (such as diversity in Chapter 7) as a current social positioning within the social structure and as an aspect that renders social inequality explorable, far from social statistical structures. These provide only a specific perspective on transformation, as can be shown by contrasting the nostalgic narratives of the former established (Chapter 7) with those of the former outsiders (Chapter 8). However, for grasping social and spatial transformations in its breadth, it is necessary to draw the attention to experiences, narratives and social positionings of various social groups.

Notes

1 In recent decades there has been a significant increase in Germany in terms of the inequality in household income (regarding the increase between 2000 and 2017, cf. Eurostat 2019). The income inequality increased from 28.9 Gini-coefficient in 1995 to 31.9 in 2016 (Gini-coefficient in the UK is 34.8). The Gini index measures the distribution of income (a higher index means higher inequality within an economy) (World Bank 2020). Poverty rate (ratio of the number of people whose income falls below the poverty line) increased from 0.090 in 2008 to 0.104 in 2017 (poverty rate in the UK is 0.119) (OECD 2020). This increase in the relative poverty rate can be partly explained by a rise in atypical employment with part-time and mini-jobs, and also by an increase in high incomes. Simultaneously, the property inequality has risen (Grabka and Westermeier 2014). While the poorest 50% of the population have only a 2.26% share of the entire net household wealth of Germany in 2014, the richest 5% of the population have approximately 51.5%, the top 1% of households own a third and only 400 households (the richest 0.001%) own 4.67% of the total wealth of Germany – twice as much as the entire poorer half of households (20 million households) (Bach, Thiemann and Zucco 2018). Overall, social advancement has become more difficult to achieve, and according to Groh-Samberg (2008), class boundaries have become harder to overcome.

2 Emotions, affect and feelings are different. Feelings are a personal articulation which is biographically related to a person's past experiences. Emotions are the outward display of those feelings and are social events, while effect is an unconscious spontaneous pre-linguistic feeling which is trigged by factors that are out of our control (Massumi 1987: ix–xx). This happens less in non-narrated situations, and more during immediate body engagements. Non-representational theory focusses particularly on effect. This book focusses on the narrated experience, and so is about feelings expressed as emotions during biographically related narrations.

3 Many investigations can be taken as an example of this. Based on data from SOEP (sozio-ökonomisches Panel), Frick and Grabka (2009) show in retrospect the development of the inequality of assets in Germany, and also the frequently cited study by Thomas Piketty demonstrates an increase in inequality in the distribution of wealth since the 18th century, based on historical statistical data sources (Piketty 2014).

4 Elias shows that an I-identity as reflexively constructed and presented in biographical narratives (Giddens 1994) always goes hand in hand with a we-identity. Even if the relationship between I-identity and we-identity may change in the process of civilisation, nonetheless there will not be a dissolution (Elias 2001).

5 Assmann conceptualised Halbwachs' concept of cultural memory further by considering a difference between communicative and cultural memory. While communicative memory is only common memory through everyday life communication, cultural memory is the specific knowledge that is learnt and expanded upon from generation to generation and that navigates activities and experiences (Assmann 2006).

6 In 2016 the number of workers in the total work population amounted to 7.7 million people (Bundesanstalt für Arbeitsschutz und Arbeitsmedizin 2018).

7 For Pierre Nora, memorial sites are not limited to physical places, but among others also encompass imaginations, memorial days, songs or literature.

8 Like Elias, Pierre Bourdieu in his concept of habitus (1984) and Anthony Giddens in his theory of structuration (1988) have emphasised that society and individual must be conceived of in relation to one another.

9 South Nuremberg is the area south of the main station and the railroad embankment. It is a transformed industrial area of different city quarters that includes factory sites, office buildings, apartment blocks and in the outskirts also some detached houses.

10 Winston Parva is a pseudonym for a suburb of the British City of Leicester.

11 At this point I prefer to not delve more deeply into the concept of the established and the outsiders; it will be exemplified by Werderau, a district of South Nuremberg, in detail in Chapter 7.

12 In their study on the iron and steel industry and the image of the worker in society, Popitz et al. 1957 point to a rudimentary collective consciousness of the working class particularly characterised as a social positioning at the "bottom" as opposed to at the "top." Later Kern and Schumann (1970) show an internal fragmentation of the industrial workforce resulting from the now more differentiating work challenges as a result of partial automation and rationalisation. In another later study by Kern and Schumann (1984) this internal fragmentation of the workforce has grown further as a consequence of newly introduced production concepts (see Dörre, Happ and Matuschek 2013 for an overview).

13 With the New Working Class Studies which stand in the tradition of cultural studies and work with ethnographic methods, this is different in the USA and in Great Britain (Charlesworth 2000; Russo and Linkon 2005; Mollona 2009; Rogaly and Taylor 2009; Kirk and Wall 2011; Thiel 2012; Blackshaw 2013).

14 Based on the analysis of management consultants from the 1970s and 1990s, Boltanski and Chiapello (2003) verify in their study a change in the spirit of capitalism. In his "Protestant Ethic" Weber argued that capitalism had developed into a "shell as hard as steel" (Weber 2015 [1904/1905]: 203). Based on that, Boltanski and Chiapello diagnosed a change in the spirit of capitalism that gives the pursuit of profit an ethical foundation. The early criticism of capitalism regarding alienated work was incorporated into a new spirit of capitalism. With this, the criticism ("artists' critique") of a suppressed individuality within the factory discipline allowed the development of a new spirit of capitalism demanding among other things, employees' flexibility, network formation and self-organisation within a "project-based polis."

15 In a historical review on the transformation of wage labour and social security, Castel indicates that today's work society is segmented in three zones: the secure zone of integration losing significance (this includes persons in formally secure working conditions), the zone of precariousness gaining in significance (refers to those working in insecure forms of employment and low-wage jobs) and the hopeless zone of isolation (refers to those permanently excluded from regular employment) (Castel 2000).

16 The intersectionality approach has its roots in the analysis of racism and sexism illustrated by Afro-American women in the USA (Crenshaw 1989).

Part I

Context

Spatial and social transformations

2 Field methods and the local context

The location of interviews is important as it constructs the positionality of the participants and produces "'micro-geographies' of spatial relations and meaning" (Elwood and Martin 2000: 649). This is true for the interview site – the living room or restaurant – where the researcher and the interviewees meet. Here social interactions and power relations between both are of relevance for the course of the conversation (Frers and Meier 2021). But the interviewees narration is also affected by the city where the interviews took place (Nuremberg in Franconia).

As products of ongoing practices, cities are always under transformation, which can be seen at different levels, such as in social structures, local economies and politics, architecture and materiality, cultural products, social encounters and social identities. The city's history is still of relevance in the structures of Nuremberg and can be seen in its architecture, for example, in streets that follow ancient routes through the city, in old premises or transformed buildings that refer to former structures. Nuremberg's past is also of relevance in today's narratives and memories of the interviewees. This is reflected in a specific dialect (formed as a mixture of the dialects of settlers from the Upper Palatinate and those from Franconia) and also by the contextualisations of individual's or family histories within the history of the city. With its long history of industry, Nuremberg has attained a specific imprint that is as a local "structure of feeling" (Williams 1977) relevant for interviewees today. The "structure of feeling" approach (see Chapter 1) connects contemporary structures and practices in Nuremberg with "residual" and "emergent" structures. Consequently, it provides a perspective on the past as being relevant for today. To understand the narratives of workers and their experiences of social inequality, as examined in this book, the history and transformations of Nuremberg, where the interviews took place, must be explained.

The functions of this chapter are twofold. First, it presents the methods used in fieldwork and especially in taking biographic interviews in the local context of Nuremberg. Second, the chapter provides the history of the local context. This is relevant for understanding today's "structure of feeling" and for understanding the context in which the workers' coping strategies – in terms of changes in their social positions – are interpreted in later chapters.

Field methods

The empirical data in this book are based on various sources collected in the course of the research project SPHERE ("Space, Place and the Historical and Contemporary Articulations of Regional, National and European Identities through Work and Community in Areas undergoing Economic Restructuring and Regeneration").[1] The main body of the data was collected from 25 biographical interviews with males and females who work or have worked in South Nuremberg and who are still living in the area. In addition, data were also collected from ten expert interviews, a focussed ethnography (Knoblauch 2005) of the interview location, secondary data analyses and two focus group interviews (each with three to five industrial workers).

Each of the interview quotes in this book is accompanied by specific information about the interviewee's age, gender, job and employer. Interviews were primarily focussed on older industrial workers, mainly from metalworking and electrical professions. By the term, "older" interviewees, this book refers to people over the German retirement age (65 years). The 25 biographical interviews were held with 13 respondents over 65 years old. These participants refer in the narratives to their own experiences from the past, mainly since the 1950s. The other 12 interviewees included three under 35 years old, four between 35 and 50 years old and five between 50 and 65 years old, who refer in the narratives to their past and recent experiences. Some interviewees have experienced unemployment due to plant closures or have changed their employer for other reasons. In addition to those who were receiving a regular pension (being older than 65 years old), some had retired early because of ill health.

All the interviewees have been employed as skilled and experienced workers. Some started unskilled, but qualified further during their working lives. Others were skilled manual workers when they started. Especially those with personal migration experience – five of the interviewees: three from Turkey, one from Spain and one from the German Democratic Republic (GDR) – started as unskilled workers and gained qualifications during their working lives. Most interviewees are working or have worked in large industrial companies in Nuremberg like Maschinenfabrik Augsburg-Nürnberg Aktiengesellschaft [MAN], Allgemeine Elektrizitäts-Gesellschaft [AEG], Grundig or Siemens. Some were or are employed in smaller metalworking companies or car repair shops. During their working lives, some interviewees have also worked outside Nuremberg: for example, some who worked at the Maxhütte in Sulzbach-Rosenberg moved to Nuremberg after its closure. As the Maxhütte was pre-eminent in the biographical narratives for these interviewees and they are still visiting the site from Nuremberg, this 50 km distant location is also included in the analyses of interview data and discussion of findings.

Interviewees had experienced job changes and plant closures, which are still significant today in their biographic memories and sometimes they visit their previous places of employment. Most of the factories of relevance in the interviewees' narratives are located or were located before their closure in South Nuremberg, for example, plants like MAN, Siemens and Grundig. AEG is located in West Nuremberg: interviewees who refer to their working life in AEG live in South Nuremberg and also have work experience in factories in South Nuremberg (Table 2.1).

The collection process, the sample selection and the analysis follow the principles of a constructivist approach (Charmaz 2014) of grounded theory (Strauss and Corbin 1994). This means that along with the principle of openness in the course of the research process (both during data collection and analysis), a theory was developed based on the collected data. Data collection and analysis were not separated from one another as completed phases, and (as in the constructivist approach of the grounded theory) the researcher was a serious and crucial part of the research process.

The contact with the interviewees to arrange for the biographical interviews was established in different ways: through the trade union, a sports

Table 2.1 Industrial plants with a specific relevance in the interviewees' narratives

Company	*Products*	*Development*	*Location in Nuremberg*
Herkules	Bicycles and motorbikes	Factory closure in Nuremberg in 1999 Completely demolished Now the area includes a car wash business	Southwest
Grundig	Consumer electronics	Insolvency and divestiture in 2003 / final closure in 2016 Loss of about 1300 jobs Partly reused for offices and advanced vocational training	Southeast
AEG	Electrical equipment	Closed in 2007 Loss of about 1700 jobs Now the area is reused by smaller productions, offices, trade, restaurants and art	West
MAN	Mechanical engineering, engines	Large industrial area partly decreased Today with about 4100 jobs	South
Siemens	Engines, gears, transformers, logistics, engineering, etc.	Former Schuckert company merged with Siemens	South
Maxhütte	Steel works	Closure in 2002 About 5000 jobs in the 1960s Now partly a ruin, but with a running pipe plant (450 employees)	In the city of Sulzbach-Rosenberg, 50 km to the East

club (which has a deep-rooted tradition as a workers' sports club), advertisement in a housing cooperative newsletter, through the city administration involved in the project "Social City," and finally through snowball sampling following the interviews.

I allowed the interviewees to select their preferred location for the interview. The biographical interviews mostly took place in interviewees' apartments or houses; only a few were interviewed in restaurants or in the offices of companies.

The biographical interviews consisted of multiple interview sessions with an overall duration of three to seven hours. They were structured and divided into three phases (entry story, inquiry phase with respect to the entry story and inquiry phase with respect to topics not yet addressed) (Schütze 1983). Following a stimulation to tell one's life story from the beginning, the interviewees developed a self-dynamic narrative, which I initially did not interrupt. In such impromptu narratives the interviewees came up with a story with which they enter into a consistent reproduction and reflexion of former experiences. Being swept up in the process of storytelling[2], a self-dynamic narrative process develops (Schütze 1983) in which certain events are either suppressed or emphasised and where one's own life story takes on a tellable logic.

Further, two focus group interviews were conducted. In the first focus group, three workers and members of a sports club (two males and one female) participated and in the second focus group, five male ex-MAN workers (all over 60 years old) participated. The focus group format differed from the biographical interviews in that the interviewees referred directly to the prior narratives of other participants. In consequence, common experiences and memories are evoked much more.

Local context and its transformation

With around half a million inhabitants, Nuremberg is the second largest city in Bavaria. Nuremberg has a long history, with the first documented mention of the city dating back to 1050. The core of its development was the imperial castle still visible on a hill at the centre of the city. The significance of the city of Nuremberg and its castle increased during the period of the Hohenstaufen, with the castle regularly accommodating kings and emperors. Today, the castle is a landmark, a tourist destination and a museum, and the castle complex is used for festivals, music concerts, open-air cinema and sports events (Figure 2.1).

Its central location on trade routes helped to foster the growth of Nuremberg in the middle ages, making the city wealthy. During this period the trade of metal crafts and textiles produced in Nuremberg were especially important to the city's economic success. Many merchants were also active in mining and finance. After the Thirty Years' War (1618–1648), Nuremberg lost some of its economic importance. The population and number

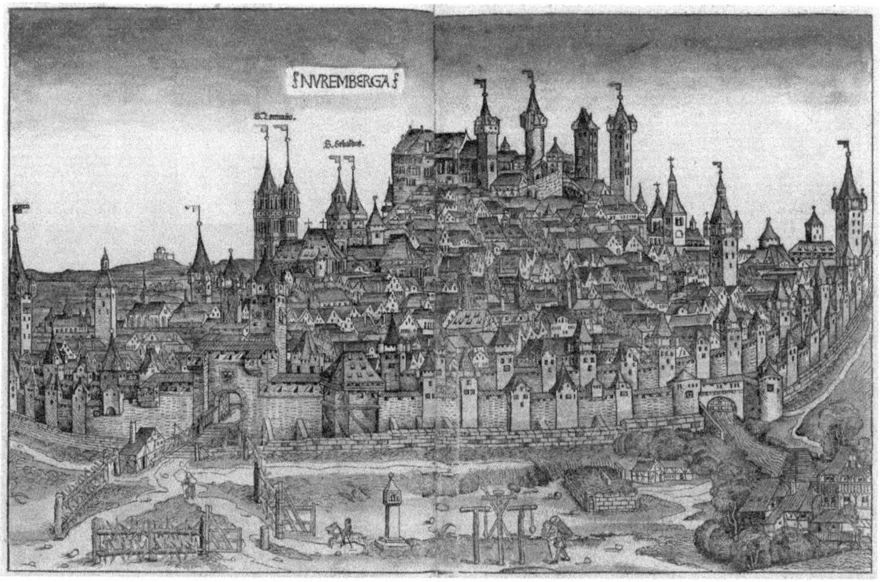

Figure 2.1 Oldest printed view of Nuremberg, Schedelsche Weltchronik, 1493, public domain, https://commons.wikimedia.org/w/index.php?curid=298410.

of handicraft businesses declined, but the city continued to be an important centre for trade into the 18th century, with an export-oriented economy of metal products, tools for drawing, textiles, mirrors, toys and more (Diefenbacher 2010). With the advent of industrialisation, some of the former craft shops developed into industrial companies. The establishment of the iron foundry and machine factory Klett & Co between 1837 and 1842, together with other companies (like Spaeth & Co), is an example of the early phases of industrialisation in Nuremberg. Later, Klett & Co became Maschinenfabrik Augsburg-Nürnberg Aktiengesellschaft (MAN), which, in 1913, was the largest employer in Bavaria. The electrical industry was also substantial, with companies like AEG and the Schuckert company (electric railway engineering and arc lamps), which later merged to become Siemens-Schuckert AG (Braun 2007). Most notably, Germany's first railway line (1835), which ran the Adler between Fürth and Nuremberg, is proof of the city's prominence during the industrial revolution (Figure 2.2).

Industrialisation transformed the economy and the shape of Nuremberg, with a 773% growth in the number of inhabitants between 1811 and 1910 (to 333,000 inhabitants; Krapf 2013) and by incorporating districts like Gostenhof or Wöhrd. At the beginning of industrialisation, workers lived near the castle in poor and crowded quarters with very low hygiene and housing standards. Later, with the foundation of housing cooperatives like the Nürnberger Wohnungsbauverein (1918) and the Bauverein Schuckert`scher

Figure 2.2 The first German train "Adler" in 1835, salt print, in the public domain, https://commons.wikimedia.org/w/index.php?curid=8730959.

Arbeiter (1896), better living conditions were secured with new apartment buildings and quarters (like Werderau and Gartenstadt) in South Nuremberg (Meier and Promberger 2012).

In addition, pubs and sport clubs were established as important places for workers to spend their leisure time. Because of strong labour movements, trade unions, and leftist labour parties (KPD and SPD), before 1933, Nuremberg was called the "red" working-class city. During the regime of the Nazi party, which received wide support in the city, however, Nuremberg became the site of the annual Nazi party congress and the staging for the propaganda movies of Leni Riefenstahl. The Nürnberger Gesetze, the pseudo-juridical laws deprived Jews and other groups of their civil rights, were proclaimed in Nuremberg. Besides its wartime manufacturing, Nuremberg was a central transportation hub, and the city was heavily damaged by bombings in 1945.

Signs of Industrialisation and the Nazi era are still visible in the infrastructure of the city, on street names, and at some heritage sites like industrial museums, monuments to company founders, and in the Documentation Center Nazi Party Rally Grounds museum.

For some of the older interviewees (defined as "older" if over the German retirement age), the period of destruction at the end of the war was the beginning of their biographic narratives. However, only some experienced the end of the Second World War; the next phase, economic recovery, which occurred in the 1950s, was a much more prominent feature in many of the interviewees' narratives.

Industry in Nuremberg was always (and still is) heavily involved in weapons manufacture, including submarine engines, trucks and other military equipment used in both world wars. After the war, large and prominent

Nuremberg companies played a role in the so-called economic miracle (*Deutsches Wirtschaftswunder*), especially those in the metalworking and engineering sectors (e.g. AEG, MAN, Grundig, Diehl, Triumph Adler, and Siemens) as well as smaller firms. The reconstruction of destroyed buildings and infrastructure (see Figure 2.3) also drove economic growth. In the 1950s, completely new districts of apartment blocks for war refugees and workers, such as Langwasser, were built, and the nearly completely destroyed old city core from the middle ages was rebuilt.

Since the 1950s, the German welfare state further expanded its benefits, including unemployment and health insurance. This was accompanied by a general rise in wages and pensions, strong labour unions and low unemployment rates. With a general rise of mass purchasing power, more social security for workers and Taylorist mass production, the post-war period industry has been labelled Fordist (Hirsch and Roth 1986).

Because of low unemployment rates and a high demand for labour beginning in the 1960s, there has been a continuous inflow of migrants to Nuremberg. Since then, not only has the number of people with a migrant background from the former recruitment countries of Turkey, the former Yugoslavia, Greece, Spain and Italy increased, but, over time, there has been a greater diversity in the countries of origin. Overall, the percentage of the Nuremberg population that does not have a German passport increased from 47,877 (9.6%) in 1975 to 121,952 (23.4%) in 2018 (the total population of Nuremberg in 2018 was 535,746). In 2018, 45.9% of Nuremberg

Figure 2.3 Memorial plaque on an apartment block in South Nuremberg saying that the apartments were destroyed during the Second World War and rebuilt in 1958–1959 (photo taken by Lars Meier).

citizens had a migrant background, coming mainly from the former Soviet Union, Romania, Turkey, the former Yugoslavia or Greece (Stadt Nürnberg 1977; Stadt Nürnberg 2019c). In Germany, anyone who has either migrated of their own accord or whose parents were migrated is described as having "a migrant background." In the south in particular, the percentage of people with a migrant background is above average for Nuremberg. South Nuremberg is also characterised by roughly average rates of unemployment and poverty (Stadt Nürnberg 2015). The nature of industrial labour there has changed, and the lifestyle and culture of the people has become more diverse, as in other German cities (Wise and Velayutham 2009). The increased social diversity is also due to the diversification of migrants' countries of origin, and Nuremberg can even be considered super-diverse (Vertovec 2007; Wessendorf 2013).

Since the late 1960s, the number of workers in industry has begun to decline gradually due to a general shift towards the service sector, automatisation and outsourcing. This change is coincident with a long-lasting employment crisis in Germany. Since the 1980s in particular, structural changes have had significant consequences in Nuremberg. While some large-scale industrial factories closed (e.g. Herkules, AEG, and Grundig) and manufacturing jobs have been lost, new jobs have been created in the rising service sector. In addition to the restructuring of manufacturing creating more service-sector positions, new service industries have developed, including insurance companies (Nürnberger Versicherungsgruppe), logistics, consumer research (GfK) and the IT sector (DATEV). Concurrently, the structure of the working population underwent a change with the expansion of the service sector, creating more white-collar jobs and decreasing the number of blue-collar jobs. The dominant metalworking and electronic industries in Nuremberg have more than halved since the 1970s, and the employment rate in manufacturing decreased from 139,120 persons in 1974 to 78,209 in 1998 and 62,105 in 2017. Employment in the service sector climbed from 131,386 persons in 1974 to 176,000 in 1998 and 245,646 in 2017. Besides changes in the economic sectors, the number of employees and workers has also changed.

In Germany, the term employees ("Angestellte") refers mainly to those who perform primarily intellectual work (white-collar workers), while the term workers ("Arbeiter/Arbeiterin") refers to those who perform chiefly physical work (blue-collar workers). While 151,379 persons were considered workers in 1974, this number dropped to 96,459 in 2002 and 90,279 in 2004. Simultaneously, the numbers of employees increased from 125,004 persons in 1974 to 167,195 in 2002 and 163,249 in 2004 (after 2004 there is no statistical data differentiating between workers and employees; Stadt Nürnberg 1977; 2007; 2015; 2019b). In general, the number of jobs for unskilled workers has decreased while the number of jobs in the service sector and IT sector has increased. This has been accompanied by an increase in the number of employees with higher education. These structural changes took place against the backdrop of privatisations of former state-owned operations like the local railway network in 2016, the housing company GBW in 2013 and a company-owned housing cooperative in 1998 (Werderau, see Chapters 7 and 8). There were cuts and restrictions in welfare support and structural changes in social policy, exemplified by the Hartz IV reform in 2005, a general change "from a 'caring welfare state' of the post-war years to the 'activating state' of today" (Lessenich 2008, translation by Lars Meier).

Currently, individuals are more often forced to be active and became "entrepreneurial self's" (Bröckling 2016). In consequence, a feeling of insecurity regarding social status has reached the middle classes (Koppetsch 2013), while changes in taxation have privileged large multinational companies and those with higher incomes and more property. Social inequality is rising in both Germany and Nuremberg. The structural changes to Nuremberg are also reflected by a higher than average rate of relative poverty: 21% of Nuremberg's inhabitants have an income below 60% of the average income (Stadt Nürnberg 2019b).

Gender and industrial work

Work in industrial production is a classic paradigm of men's work, and it is repeatedly described as such in the biographical interviews. This is despite the fact that women have always been employed in the industrial sector and as many as 13,000 women worked in production in Nuremberg in 2008. Even in German industrial sociology, "industrial work (...) is unfailingly defined as men's work – although several sectors with repetitive work had opened for women as well due to Taylorism/Fordism" (Schumann 2000: 107, translation by Lars Meier). Women's work in factories has always conflicted with and fundamentally challenged the dominant stereotypes about women. This is because women who have worked in the industrial sector earned their own money early in life. They were at the factory from their youth onwards so they had no time to learn household activities. With paid work, they were relatively autonomous and had some financial independence (Weyrather 2003). Overall, there is a difference between the prevailing stereotype and the empirical reality of women's work, which has a long tradition. Even during the time of National Socialism, when the Nazi regime pursued the propagandistic objective of excluding women from the working life and re-establishing them in the domestic sphere, women's employment rate rose in the industrial sector as a consequence of the wartime economy (Herbst 1982; Hachtmann 1993). In the course of the war in particular, as Sebastian Haffner noted, "never did so many women enter into so many men's work positions or functions as in World War II, and this development proved to be irreversible" (Haffner 1981: 44ff., translated by Lars Meier).

Women have always done a significant amount of wage work. However, the classic stereotype of work distribution between the genders, i.e. the men doing wage work and the women doing unpaid reproduction work at home, seems to have changed further with the progressive integration of women into paid employment, which has gone hand in hand with the extension of child care and more precarious and flexible work models in the last few decades. Correspondingly, the percentage of women employees subject to social insurance contributions has increased in the last decades in Nuremberg from 40.7% in 1980 to 45.9% in 2017. Women's employment increased from 114,110 women in 2010 to 140,665 in 2017. This trend was not accompanied by a reduction in men's employment (which also increased) (Stadt Nürnberg 2019a). However, there is consistent inequality in the employment situation of men and women. In comparison to the employment situation of men, women do less wage work on average, exhibit an above-average tendency to work in the service sector, do more part-time work and altogether earn less money. The share of part-time employees rose in Germany from 4.2 million women in 2007 to 7.1 million in 2017 (7.8 million are employed full time). Additionally, the part-time work of men rose from 0.9 million in 2007 to 1.9 million in 2017 (15.4 million men are employed full time), but the difference is striking, with a much higher number of women employed part time (Bundesagentur für Arbeit 2018). The median gross monthly salary in Nuremberg demonstrated a gender pay gap of 17.8% for full-time employees subject to social insurance contributions in 2016. Where men earn 3.671 euro, women make only 3.019 euro (Fuchs 2018). It is important to note that this difference refers only to men and women employed full time. However, if we consider that more women work part time, the total gender pay gap is much higher.

In recent years, rising women's employment in Nuremberg has been accompanied by a general extension of public childcare. Day-care centres have grown, and the number of children in nursery school under the age of three has increased heavily from 175 (1997) to 3.850 (2017). However, almost all children in their first three years of life are still taken care of at home – by their mother in most cases; only 24.7% are brought to day-care facilities (Stadt Nürnberg 2018b). Outside employment means a double burden for most of the interviewed women. This is because in addition to paid work, many women bear the main responsibility for housework and parenting (Lott 2019). One woman, born in 1962, who worked as an assembler of printed circuit boards at Grundig [manufacturer of consumer electronics], said:

> As a woman, it's not easy. Work, parenting, household chores, still shift work. It wasn't easy.

Conclusion

Today, despite its structural transformations and an increase in service-sector work (together with more diversity, changes in gender relations, more precarious labour relations and an increase in social inequalities) Nuremberg still has a very important industrial sector. Its long history as an important industrial city has left a lasting imprint on Nuremberg. As will be demonstrated in the following chapters, this imprint, which can be considered a specific "local structure of feeling" (Taylor, Evans and Fraser 1996), is also relevant to the class identity of today's workers. It is obvious (as demonstrated in Chapters 7 and 8) that besides the workplace especially the area of residence has relevance in the narrated memories of the interviewees.

Notes

1 SPHERE is a cooperation project sponsored by the EU as part of the 7th framework programme (FP7-2007-SSH8-5.2.01) with the following partner institutions: Middle East Technical University in Ankara; London Metropolitan University; Universidad Complutense de Madrid; Uniwersytet Slaski, Institut für Arbeitsmarktforschung (IAB).

2 Characteristics of the impromptu narratives are: (1) The competence of being able to decide whether a narrative is completed in its form (obligation to complete the story); (2) The limitation and compression of the narrative (obligation to condense the story); (3) Detailing the narrative for plausibility reasons (obligation to detail the story) (Schütze 1983).

3 Transformations of class

Class is the outcome of an internally unequal society that is structured by social factors such as power and the possession of economic, symbolic, social or cultural capital. Class defines one's position in the social structure and intersects with other factors, such as gender, "ethnicity" and age. It is repeatedly re-established by means of everyday cultural practices, such as the furnishing of one's home, or through certain forms of everyday activities, such as one's way of dressing, eating or moving and one's way of presenting one's body or using it for work. However, a person's class is not expressed only, for example, by the tin plates on the wall (Figure 3.1) featuring congratulations from colleagues about one's work jubilee; class can also be expressed by taking a certain perspective in interviews. Like "doing gender" (West and Zimmerman 1987), "doing class" (Yodanis 2006; Scharff 2008) correspondingly occurs also in the attribution of abilities, which the interviewees ascribed to a group of other people and which either corresponded to their self-attributed abilities or were presented in contrasting terms as the distinctive abilities of other classes. The interviewees constructed the self and the other via such actual or attributed cultural practices.

Class is not always expressed as a collective awareness of a shared social position resulting in collective interests. A "class in itself" does not necessarily become self-aware as a "class for itself" (Marx 1847). Although there are indications of such awareness in some of the interviews, it is obvious that the narrated life stories are constructions of a personal individuality. This is because the inference of common life styles, behaviours or interests from any class puts into doubt individual authenticity and is therefore in constant contradiction to the powerful social discourse of individual freedom and self-fulfilment (Savage 2005). Thus, it is not surprising that the interviewees did not directly relate their own lifestyles, everyday practices or experiences to any social class position except in rare cases. However, an analysis of their narratives makes this relation evident. This is different from gender because the interviewees frequently referred their behaviours, views or experiences in relation to their gender, which is actively re-constructed and performed through such narratives (Butler 1993).

Although the interviewees did not directly use the term "class," dimensions of class are present in various ways in the interviews and in the field observations in South Nuremberg. Class is regarded in this book as a

Figure 3.1 Tin plate with congratulations about the 40th work jubilee (photo taken by Lars Meier).

category of social science, which did not have to be named directly by the interviewees but can be inferred – a task for the social scientist – from the data collected from the interviews.

Transformations and learning class

The life story interviews show that class affiliation is continually assimilated and assigned in a social learning process. In this context, early life experiences play an especially important role and are repeatedly referred to in biographical interviews. The ensuing social self-placements are an answer to the question, "Which skills do I have, and which skills do I lack?" In the interviews, the answer to this question can often be derived from childhood experiences. Presumed skills are repeatedly assigned from the family, at school, during vocational guidance or apprenticeship assignment.

Through a learning process those attributed skills are accompanied by self-attributions. The attribution of abilities at school or other institutions, such as an employment agency, is of great significance and has consequences for one's whole life. Today's employees in the industrial sector had to learn early that other people (e.g. teachers) are empowered to assess them and that the respective assessments have far-reaching consequences for their lives, or, as Sennett and Cobb put it, "The badges of ability seem unfairly awarded, yet hard to repudiate" (1972: 118). One toolmaker, who was born in 1928, narrated how his entrance into the world of work was determined by other people:

> Together with my mother, I went to the employment agency [1943]. It was very difficult to find a place of apprenticeship because there were hardly any training positions. Just as it is today. And then he produced a list with remaining options, looked at me and simply said: wouldn't that be quite the thing for him, toolmaker. And my mother immediately agreed. After all, she was glad that I even got an apprenticeship. (...) I didn't know anything about it.

A foundry mechanic, who was born in 1952, told me that his occupational career was influenced by conflicts with the school principal, causing him to drop out without an intermediate school degree.

> After the 6th grade, I went to an intermediate school. Um...after two years...um...I was fed up with intermediate school. This was very much related to the principal or to the vice-principal of that time, who was also a nasty piece of work in my opinion. Besides me, there were several others who dropped out – personalities who didn't necessarily say yes and OK to everything.

In 1977, Paul Willis examined how class is learnt at school. His study shows how "working class kids get working class jobs" as a consequence of learning certain cultural practices. Willis describes how juveniles with a working-class background use various day-to-day practices to express their opposition to the values of the middle class, such as conformity and a belief in the importance of formal education. This not only involves the process of self-allocation to the working class together with the formation of the corresponding habitus (Bourdieu 1984) but tragically also means that these juveniles block their own upward social mobility into the middle class. The fact that class is learnt at school can also be shown by means of the interviews that were conducted in South Nuremberg. In this context, the gender-specific differentiations and the interwovenness of the identity dimensions of class and gender are revealed as well. Unlike in the case of men, the opposition behaviour of the interviewed women was expressed more by passive resistance. Similar to the observations of Paul Willis, several of the male workers talked about their opposition behaviour at school, about being a personality "who does not necessarily say yes and OK to everything" and about other forms of rebellious behaviour. These forms of behaviour, including active and passive rebelliousness (see Chapter 6), now serve the interviewees as the reasons for their school performance and their subsequent occupational career. One metal worker, who was born in 1973, remembered that in his childhood, he was a "troublemaker" who did "a lot of mischief" in the south of the city. Unlike the active rebelliousness of the young men, two of the interviewed women (a 42-year-old retail saleswomen and a 58-year-old former warehouse clerk) presented their more passively recalcitrant practices as an explanation for the end of their school career after finishing lower secondary school and for their subsequent career as workers.

> I only attended lower secondary school, I was so, so idle.
> I was just a bit lazy there, I must honestly admit.

Today, however, it seems that some things have changed. In contrast to Willis' study and the life stories of the interviewees – in which the self-confident rebellious practices of future workers were recounted – the confidence of juveniles upon becoming future members of the working class has obviously evaporated. In an expert interview a school social worker said that today's students at lower secondary school behave in a much more conformist or – in the words of the social worker – in a more resigned way than they did in the past. Unlike in former times, when a certificate of lower secondary education was an entrance card to a self-confident work force and when rebellious practices at school represented a cultural act of self-assignment to the working class, nowadays, mere attendance at lower secondary school no longer opens the promising prospect of becoming an established worker. Today, the students consider their placement at a lower secondary school as a manifestation of their failure, and – unlike in the past – they no longer regard it as the start of a career as a craftsman or skilled worker.

The narratives of the older interviewees illustrate that the significance of the school career for one's integration into the working world has changed. Their stories of the school experiences seem, in part, almost casual in character, and their school attendance was often fragmentary or lasted only a few years due to the war. Particularly striking in these interviews was the change in parents' expectations: in the past, parents who were workers themselves preferred that their children graduate from school early to become apprentices and earn money for the family. From this point of view, the school-leaving certificate or the duration of the school education was almost irrelevant if one wanted to get a job as a worker. One trained engraver, who was born in 1932, narrated the following:

> At seven years to primary school. Um...this was primary school from 1939 to 1943. Then, from 1943 to 1946 at higher secondary school. One Monday, I arrived at school and – to my surprise – the teacher said to

> me: "why are you here today, you have to do an admission test for higher secondary school." Well, I didn't know. So he had registered an application for me because of my grades. My father was away fighting in the war, and my mother worked at a factory. And then this, this notification…um…somehow was lost. Or my mother didn't think it important enough. Or she thought I knew. Anyway, I went there and did the admission test, which I passed. (…) I continued to attend higher secondary school, although my parents were actually opposed to this. Again, my teacher pushed this through. Because my brother already had an apprenticeship. So he brought home some money. And I was the one on whom money was spent. Because of this, I finally dropped out on my own account after three years at that school. On that day, I just didn't go to school and went to the education authority instead. I registered back to the old school. (…) Well, I said, I won't leave from there anymore. I will go back to primary school because I was under such a pressure, primarily from my father, to work instead of going to school. Well, so I went back to primary school.

The biographical story of an electrician and transport worker, born in 1938, also revealed that the school-leaving certificate was not considered relevant for one's further career as a worker.

> In 1949 (…) I left school. Primary school, 7th grade. I could have done 8th grade there. But I was allowed to leave at 7th grade because I practically missed one year of school in this rural area. And my mother said I should start an apprenticeship at 14. And then I trained three and a half years as a mechanic and lathe operator and completed my apprenticeship in 1953.

After the war, school was not important to worker boys and girls as an institution at which they could obtain education qualifications to acquire the necessary institutionalised cultural capital (Bourdieu 1984) for entrance into the work force. Independent of success at school, integration into the workforce was largely mediated by the attribution and acquisition of certain abilities, such as being practical, which will be looked at in more detail in the next section. In these stories, the integration into the working class is not described as a consequence of any success at school but rather as a chronological inevitability: after completing or dropping out of school, young people started an apprenticeship and were thus integrated into the work force. However, there is a noticeable change of perspective within the biographical stories. In contrast to the remembered perspective of their parents, the interviewees found it particularly important that their own children attain as high an educational level as possible. Their perspective on the occupational careers of their offspring was radically different from their perspective on their own career. This can be shown by the biographical story of a female laboratory assistant and storekeeper who was born in 1952:

> When we were young the...um...the qualified certificate and all that didn't even exist. You went to primary school and then you switched, you got an apprenticeship. And, well, that was just the normal thing at that time. (...) How I now try to hammer this into my nephews over and over, I say look here! (Taps with her fingers on the table top.) Pay attention to this, you must learn, you must. One of them now attends grammar school. I hope he will say at some time in the future, even if you just have your diploma from grammar school, you have it, you have got something. Nowadays, if you haven't got anything to show, if you only have a certificate of lower secondary education or the like, then you are in a fine kettle of fish. You simply don't have any career chances.

From the perspective of the workers, their own educational career, which provided them entrance into the established working class, can no longer be used as a model for young people. What in parents' minds had been enough to get a recognised job as a worker and be socially integrated, i.e. just minimal presence at school, has now been replaced by the objective of enabling one's own children and grandchildren to attain as high an educational level as possible. From the viewpoint of the workers, the promise of social integration by means of one's school and career path – lower secondary school (or primary school), apprenticeship, occupation – can no longer be trusted.

The interviewees considered their offspring's placement at a secondary school not so much a means of social advancement as it is part of the effort to keep one's present level in society and prevent one's offspring from being "in a fine kettle of fish" after school. In contrast to how the older interviewees themselves were treated by their parents, the interviewees now further the school careers of their offspring and are proud of the assistance they provide in acquiring educational qualifications. A former female employee, born in 1966, who has worked as a salesperson and kitchen assistant in the AEG factory canteen, said the following:

> If I look at my daughter, she is now almost 24. She studies at university, she'll complete her studies in spring; she studies pharmacy. Um, this makes me very proud, actually. Yes, and my second eldest, Ansgar, now also goes to grammar school. 7th grade. And the little one, well, he goes to lower secondary school. Not everyone is the same, after all, well. But you always try hard to ensure that all your children find their own path. In some way or other. And if I actually see it happening, this makes me proud, actually.

Practical knowledge and transformations of the habitus

All of the interviewees, irrespective of age and work sector, described themselves as highly industrious; in their biographical narratives, they spoke of the tasks they carry out in their private life in addition to their wage work, which they execute with commitment. The self-attribution of properties such as idleness and laziness only occurred in connection with the interviewees' performance at educational institutions. With respect to their subsequent wage work or domestic work, the interviewees ascribed themselves exactly the opposite qualities, such as industriousness and perseverance.

This contrast in their self-description – being lazy as opposed to being industrious – corresponds to the fact that several interviewees ascribed themselves practical abilities while at the same time disclaiming any abilities that they thought of as theoretical. This self-attribution of practical abilities in combination with an acceptance of lacking theoretical abilities is at the core of working-class affiliation. The self-definition of being lazy refers to learning at school, but it no longer holds true and turns into the opposite where experience with practical work is concerned.

In the course of one's school experience, the self-definition of being a practical person (and the distaste for largely theoretical subject matter at school) is established through one's own experiences and/or through an attribution or non-attribution of abilities at school. This self-definition grows into a manifest part of one's own identity and proves to be characteristic of the working class. One mechanic and lathe operator, who was born in 1932, talked about his choice of career:

> I just wanted a practical job. Because I was a little more of a...um... somehow more of a practical person...um...than a theoretical person. Writing and the like wasn't my cup of tea. No, even at school, it wasn't my thing particularly. With respect to German school lessons, I was probably a failure.

A motor mechanic who was born in 1952 gave his practical abilities as one reason for his choice of career:

> I couldn't picture myself working, let's say, in trade or in the business sector, which would have been possible as well. I wanted to do some handicraft work. To work more with my hands, so to say.

The conviction of having the ability to perform physical labour and using one's body skilfully for practical work was a repeatedly recurring element in the stories and self-descriptions of the interviewees. On the negative side, this was accompanied by repulsion towards anything with a theoretical nature; on the positive side, the interviewees ascribed themselves the ability to perform practical work and a quick comprehension of practical work steps.

Figure 3.2 House in the Falkenheim district (photo taken by Lars Meier).

The interviewees underwent a physical learning process, with their experiences being physically inscribed and manifested in practices and in their habitus (Bourdieu 1984). There was also a simultaneous inscription into an identity-constituting self-definition as a person who is able to do practical work, in contrast to those who lack this ability. This separation between intellectual work and physical work, which was present in the interviews, is an important element for differentiation and class formation.

A 71-year-old former electrician, who once worked in the industrial sector and then in a department store, talks about his abilities, which, in his opinion, differentiated him from service-sector employees doing deskwork. As an example, he described the renovation work on his home, which he carried out by himself. The respective house is part of the Falkenheim district, which was built in a joint effort out of the remains of the bombed city in 1958 (Figure 3.2). He recounted the following:

> For instance, I just bought the windows, but installed them myself, being a craftsman, until, well, until 2007, 2008. I still installed all the plates myself, altogether 3.6 tons. Well, I even bought a mortar mixer just to prepare the mortar. And so on, yes. Then, I did shovel work at the front and at the back of the house. And I re-insulated the foundation. I did all that on my own. Well, I'm a lone fighter, you know.

Later, he continued:

> I learned those things just from observing others and I do everything by myself. The windows and the window blinds, I installed them all by myself. (...) Well, I really worked my ass off, sometimes. But you also felt happy time and again. For instance, the terrace, that's where I started, on the terrace. And then, when you have just finished the first few square meters and, well, you look back, then you see something, don't you? But somebody sitting in his office, he doesn't see anything of his work (both laugh), now, does he? Like this, well. Well, and so I carried it out.

The interviewees contrasted their own abilities with the abilities of others. The interviewed male workers defined themselves as people who have some practical knowledge, which they considered to be a result of their ability to use their body skilfully for work, and which, in their opinion, differentiates them from service-sector employees, who lack this ability and are not in intensive, direct physical contact with the products of their work. The work of the service-sector employees was described by the workers as work that is, due to its theoretical character, out of touch with reality, and hence irrelevant. In the interviews with the workers, the direct, sensory, and physical contact with the material products of their work came up over and over again as an identity-constituting element of their class affiliation that contrasted with the experiences of other classes. As the interviewee above said, "But somebody sitting in his office, he doesn't see anything of his work." On the other hand, one metal worker, who was born in 1988, characterised the result of his work as follows:

> That, firstly, you can be creative and, secondly, you can really...um... achieve something of real duration.

The self-definition of being a person with practical skills (not a theoretical person), which was formed as a result of an unsuccessful school career (Willis 1977), generated the confidence to be able to learn and carry out practical work even without the help of others. Again and again, the interviewees set out how they built their houses virtually by themselves or how they repaired cars, acquiring the necessary knowledge – apparently without any inhibitions – on their own. A trained foundry mechanic, born in 1972, narrated the following:

> Lars: And where did you pick up all these skills? You said, you converted your house yourself and...
> Martin: You just take a look, contemplate, think about it, or possibly ask someone how to do it and then just try. The first time I laid laminate flooring, a work colleague briefly showed me how it was done. At that time, you had to glue the flooring panels together. Nowadays, you use

> laminate with a locking system. Quickly done, self-explanatory, well, with a bit of practical understanding, technical knowledge. I also repair cars. In my leisure time. All my mates, many work colleagues, they all have their car serviced by me or they ask me to get it through the TÜV [mandatory safety inspection]. For this, I haven't been trained either. Everything is step-by-step.

A former metal worker (born in 1945) who was forced into his occupation by his father through beatings (his career aspiration was to become a cook) – "father always decided everything" – narrated how his occupation involved the acquisition of certain physical abilities so that he became skilful in handicrafts and could assemble some small furniture for his apartment. Under the premise that class is established, among other things, by physical practices and that the working class defines itself via direct physical contact with the work product, it follows that a change in work (e.g. a change of occupation into the service sector or exemption from work as a works council member) and the loss of direct physical experience in the production process leads to the formation of a new class affiliation.

Former experiences also leave traces in the body, in the body's senses and in unique body activities and contribute to habitus constitution. However, these traces are tested and partly transformed by new everyday activities and different regulations, processes and materiality in a changed work setting and new position in social space. Such transformations and their consequences for one's habitus are exemplified in the following section with the case of a manual worker who became an engineer and the case of an industrial worker who migrated as a farmer from Turkey to Nuremberg.

From being a manual worker to becoming an engineer: social advancement and the transformation of habitus

With a move into the service sector, the differentiation in workers' minds between meaningful practical work and theoretical work without relevance – which is an important element in the constitution of the working class – came into conflict with their new class identity as service-sector employees. The interviewees solved this conflict between their familiar attributions and their new role and class affiliation by talking about the effort they had to make and pointing out the relevance of the new work, thereby reformulating the earlier attributions that stemmed from the perspective of the worker.

An 80-year-old former electrical engineer, who gained further qualifications alongside his regular occupation and finally earned a master's degree in electrical engineering, described how his advancement into a higher class was accompanied by changes in his self-presentation. His social advancement was associated with an increased physical distance from the actual work process (here, from the oil of the hydraulic machinery) and was reflected by a change in clothing style in favour of clothes expressing this distance and thus indicating the class change.

> And then I qualified as an (snaps his fingers) engineer, in electrical engineering, and I took the examination for a master's certificate. I can even show you the newspaper, it says that I passed the examination with top marks. So I really applied myself. (…) Before, you know, I often…um… repaired hydraulic machines and the like, where there's a lot of oil. (…) But later on (laughs shortly) I was dressed in a white coat. A bit strange, isn't it? (…) Later on, I never went out without a jacket and tie.

At the same time, the change in clothes represented the desire to be seen as part of the higher classes and to legitimate his new class affiliation.

> I had a boss (…) I still remember. Diplom Ingenieur Maas. (…) Maas had an extremely spacious office. Outside, (snaps his fingers) sat his secretary. (…) If you wanted to see Maas, you had to register with him first. Then, he announced, a Mr. X wants to see you. "Yes, a moment please". And then Maas (snaps his fingers) steps in front of the mirror and adjusts his tie. Slips into his jacket. Swaggers to his great big desk, plants himself behind it. Like the emperor of China, right? And if you came in a shirt or in overalls (…) you were immediately kicked out. Then you hadn't done anything right, had you? But if you came in a jacket and tie, right? Everything was OK. And he was clothed in this manner even at the plant. Always with a hat, right? (…) Well, he influenced me in this as well. Right? So that I…um…(clears his throat) always ensured that I was appropriately clothed and so on and so on. (…) Well, I was recognized by people. I earned good money. Things were quite OK.

In retrospect, the interviewee considered the change in clothes to have been key to his professional success, a success that also gave rise to the enjoyment of some privileges. He recounted the following:

> So I wore tailor-made suits, had always a tie on. During the 27 years at Siemens. Right? Though some people were…um…shocked, right? But who cares? Who cares? I even found it quite enjoyable. (…) And I was successful at Siemens.

He continued:

> Business lunch, they called it. As for (laughs a bit) business, there wasn't much to talk about. But they had this advantage. You had a proper meal and the company paid for it. (…) I also got some advantages at the plant.

The desire to advance to a higher class and to enjoy the privileges resulting from this advancement is also an incentive for today's younger people to acquire the relevant educational certificates. One metal worker, who was born in 1988, talked about this aspiration:

> And it's quite fun doing it, I must say, even now. In the course of time, I gradually came to the decision that this wasn't, so to say, what I really wanted to do, ultimately, until the end of my working career. And then I passed my vocational diploma and thought, OK, why not study something at a university of applied sciences. At the Georg-Simon-Ohm University. Being just around the corner. But what should I study, the courses were somewhat technically oriented, but that was the direction I wanted to take, anyway. Then, I thought about it. What do you like doing, um, and where are the good career opportunities later on, so I chose engineering.

From a farmer in rural Turkey to an industrial worker in Nuremberg

Encountering a host country is a challenge even in terms of everyday life, and it is also a challenge to make oneself suitable for the specific needs of a new workplace. Working in an industry also means making oneself fit into a place with specific rules, such as specific work regulations, time rhythms, new colleagues and challenges for the body. For those who grew up in a family with a tradition of working in industry plants, this is a less demanding task than for those without a family background in industrial work. In the early stage of industrialisation, the task of adjusting oneself to the rules of industrial work was hard for those who had migrated from rural agricultural areas. However, this requirement has also had to be met by those people who have migrated to Nuremberg since the 1960s (see Chapter 2), for example, those from rural areas in Kurdistan, and by those with an academic background from elsewhere. Nedim, a 52-year-old man who came from Kurdistan as a refugee in 1980, told me about the challenge of working in a factory in South Nuremberg and about his transformations:

> Lars: How was it for you to start working in a factory?
> Nedim: For me it was really difficult to stand for 8 hours. That was horrible. Each day my legs hurt, really, everyday a terrible pain. I was happy at the end of the working day to have the chance to put my legs up for half an hour or so. I said I cannot stand for as long as this. But in the meantime, I have really I have adapted to this. Now it is no bother for me to stand for ten or twelve hours. But it was hard for me to stand on my legs. I was 22 years old and I was used to sitting the whole day at school and then from one day to the next you have to stand for 8 hours. I was not used to do so. That was difficult. I had cramps in my legs. But I have done it. How should I say, my body has gotten used to it.

Starting to work and being included in the working community also means adapting one's habits, bodily practices and other elements of everyday activities to the new demands. These necessary personal transformations to meet the demands of work had been felt by some interviewees – who have not worked as industry workers before – as a harsh transformation that transformed them into a kind of machine. Selda, a woman with a migrant background said the following about her first day at the former Grundig plant:

> I was happy to work, but on the other hand I was not sure whether I could make it. Because there were these huge machines, how can I make it? It was my first job in industrial production. (…) we worked like machines, and we had to work like a machine otherwise it would not have been possible to achieve the given goals, the given number of items. (…) The first day I was afraid that I might not make it. But as times goes by, you get used doing so.
>
> Such large machines, two or three metres high. I haven't seen such a large company in my entire life before. I said my goodness and I have to work there. That was a shock for me. (…) It was my first job in industrial production. I said to myself that this is a machine that does not stop. You have to work so fast. I said my god you have to work like a machine. (…) It was not easy.

By working in Nuremberg's industry, the habitus was confronted with different challenges. To achieve the goals of their work, they had to alter their bodies, language and habits: they had to make themselves fit into the Nuremberg industry. By doing so, their identities also transformed, from an academic or a rural worker to an industrial worker who became part of a worker community. In an historical study on working-class history in Bengal between 1890 and 1940, Dipesh Chakrabarty demonstrated a durability of habitus structures because the "class identity of the worker could never be distilled out of the pre-capitalist identities that arise from the relationship he had born into" (Chakrabarty 2000: 218). A habitus transformation is not a complete or seamless break with a former habitus. It might occur together with several irritations and a feeling of being out of place. Such complications of habitus transformation have been demonstrated in a self-reflexive way by Pierre Bourdieu (Bourdieu 2008) and by Didier Eribon (Eribon 2009).

Differences and other classes

Like gender and "ethnicity," class is a relational category, which – as described by E.P. Thompson (1978: 295–296) – cannot be defined in the abstract but only in relation to other classes. Therefore, class is essentially based on the relation between the self and the other, irrespective of whether the distribution of power and economic capital or day-to-day cultural practices are concerned. With their self-attributions and their appraisal of others, the interviewees placed themselves in a hierarchical class structure between the lower class and the upper class. Those who had worked or were working as blue- or white-collar workers ranked themselves – via the self-definition of their cultural practices – as superior to members of the lower class in the social hierarchy. This differentiation was revealed through (among other things) stigmatising attributions which constructed a dangerous or at least unpleasant class.

Class differentiation described by the interviewees was particularly striking when they talked about their experiences at the employment agency. They feel that their status and lifelong-learned class affiliation as former blue- or white-collar workers were questioned and threatened in that situation. The interviewees felt that they were put on a level with members of the lower class and demanded that their own class identity be recognised and distinguished from that of the lower class. One interviewed woman made a distinction within the group of unemployed people on the basis of their willingness to work:

> You can't just say that everyone is lazy and lives an easy life, relying on Hartz IV [basic benefits], that's not true, far from it. (...) People who really always went to work, that they are thus...just like everyone else who was never willing to work, they are placed at the same level. And that is, that won't do.

Another interviewee was incensed at the fact that his lifelong work performance was not taken into consideration in a counselling interview, and he called for a differentiation between different kinds of unemployed people at the employment office:

> Now please take a look at the people sitting opposite. I was neatly clothed, I don't drink. I don't do anything such. She's got a point, actually, there were types at the employment agency, good lord! Dirty, reeking, drunk. With a bottle of beer and so on, and they made a ruckus. Therefore, take a look at the people sitting there. And then you can appraise them, but this is the wrong way.

The relation between the workers and the chief executives of industrial companies was described by the older interviewees in terms of change. In the interviews, the bosses of today's large industrial companies were portrayed as having lost any relation to the practical work and life situation of the workers. What was generally ascribed to all service-sector white-collar workers, i.e. a lack of physical contact with the practical work, manifested itself in a particularly severe form in the company bosses. In the interviews, these bosses appeared to be aloof, inaccessible and distant from the actual work situation. Unlike the bosses of the past times, who had a more visible presence and who were, in retrospect, acknowledged as persons who had a certain sense of responsibility towards "their" blue-collar and white-collar workers, the bosses of today's large industrial companies with transnational operations appear to have no interest in the working life of "their" workers, which is, in part, due to their physical absence.

The aloofness of the actual decision makers – who do not directly face the work situation or any work conflicts because they are physically absent – is illustrated in the following description of the AEG plant closure [AEG: German producer of electrical equipment], which resulted in the laying off of the people working there. An interviewee reported that the local management, who had to announce the decision of the executive board to the employees, was not responsible for it and actually felt sorry about it, but they had to follow the instructions of the distant bosses of the transnational corporation:

> It was no easy time (…), and for sure, it wasn't for the management either. Because I'm certain that the management, who then were downstairs with us, they didn't want AEG to close either. That was just a decision up there in Stockholm. They weren't responsible for this, not really. They for sure also had a hard time. But naturally they were the… um…the target for the workforce. It's clear that nobody can always travel to Stockholm to give them (laughs) a piece of his mind up there. And therefore, everyone vented his anger on the Nuremberg management, they took the blame for it, you know.

In the stories of the older workers, there appears to have been much more direct contact between the workers and bosses in the Fordistic period after the Second World War. These bosses of the past are portrayed as equipped with the classic attributes of a patriarch who expects obedience and submission but, in return, takes responsibility for the workers and offers them support. An interviewee talked about his apprenticeship as a heating engineer in 1952:

> We worked ten hours a day, on Saturdays as well. Well, and then we went to the workshop between 12 and 2 o'clock. And next on the agenda was car washing. So we had to wash the car of the boss on top of everything. It was an old DKW car [DKW: historic German car manufacturer], 3=6, a modern car at that time. Well, and then we were paid a buck after two hours' car washing. With this money, we felt like kings. Because with this money, on Sundays, I went over to the stadium to watch the matches of the Nuremberg football club.

Another worker talked about his relationship with his former boss.

> In the first year of apprenticeship, you had to polish the boss's bicycle and the like. This was all part of your job. And the workshop, well,

> nowadays nobody does it anymore. Sweeping the floor and whatnot (laughs). Well, times were different then. But we didn't see it in this way. Things just were like that, you know. It's just how it was. Nobody dared to complain, for what could you do?

An 80-year-old man was even subjected to physical violence during his apprenticeship in electrical engineering with Siemens near the end of the Second World War, a practice by which the boss expressed his dominance over him:

> You also got slapped there. When one week had passed and you hadn't got slapped by your boss, you thought, well, it's about time now (laughing), right?

Looking back, the interviewees described the companies in which they worked for a longer period of time in terms of being a responsible family in which the company boss took on the role of some kind of father. This description was even found in the case of large companies such as MAN and its former housing estate (see Chapters 7 and 8). In their biographical stories, the interviewees often talked about their sense of belonging and their feelings of loyalty towards the company. Assuredly, they were given a very heavy workload, but the company or handicraft enterprise also took care of them in a reliable and responsible way in return. One craftsman in the fitting business, who was born in 1973, recounted his experiences:

> I did my apprenticeship here (…) in a super-cool traditional handicraft shop. A family enterprise with 150 years of tradition. With an old patriarch, who was kind at heart, but what an autocrat! You continually got slapped. (…) [Imitates the boss] "Lousy rookie, stupid asshole, tidy up at once, finish it now or else." Such words he used. You were called asshole from morning till evening. But after five minutes, the storm had passed, everything was OK again. Just as quick as it had built up, he didn't bear grudges. And that was important to me. (…) Because he taught you everything. Including things that you no longer learn nowadays. (…) A handicraft shop was a family enterprise. That was fundamental to it (…) I worked in this enterprise for 14 years. Always in the same team. We were like a family. We had strong bonds and knew that we could rely on each other. And if there was some work to be done on Sundays, we would be willing to help and he knew it. But then, it was a give and take. (…) There was a time when I wanted to buy a car, but didn't have enough money. [He imitates the boss] "If you want to buy a car, lad, come with me." In the office upstairs, he took a small box from the old secretary. It contained banknotes, the large brown ones, each worth a thousand bucks. "Lad, how much do you need?" What I needed was three and a half thousand. He gives me four. "You take it." You just work it off.

> With this, the subject was dropped. Then, I worked overtime. And after about a year (…) the boss approached me. He says, "lad, your car is paid off now. From now you work for yourself again." And I knew that his calculation was correct to the last cent. Or he even rounded down my debt. (…) But in return, he knew that he could rely on his team, on our group. On his call, you would assemble. And then you would do it. It was a whole different mind-set.

Transformations in the work situation

When looking back on the work situation of the past, the older interviewees saw their former difficulties and challenges, such as the high physical strain, the low remuneration and the experiences of physical violence from their superiors, in a more favourable light than the changed situation of today. The negative experiences of the past seemed to pale in comparison to the negative appraisal of their current work situation. Two former workers reminisced about the social relations among the workers in the past in two enterprises that have since closed down. A former worker at Herkules (bike manufacturer) recounted the following:

> It was a great atmosphere. Indeed. We were, so to say, a really big family. We were a really gigantic family, that's what we were. We all knew each other.

He continued:

> This family life, I think, was valued and maintained by the company, so they encouraged it.

A former female AEG employee pointed out that her colleagues at the AEG factory were "like a second family."

In the narratives of the interviewees, who looked back on a long life of work and experienced many changes, the changes of the last two decades in particular were redescribed in negative terms and put into contrast with their own former working experiences. The changes in the work organisation, the new types of management and the new rationalisation and technology processes were deemed to have a negative impact on the social interactions of the workers. One former metal worker, who was born in 1940, talked about the changes and consequences of the increased intensification of work and the expansion of control activities in the last 30 years:

> In the past, there were only those manual work stations, such as lathes, etc., you actually had to do a lot of manual work. And…um…that was less stressful than today. To be sure, you don't have to do as much manual work today, you do more control activities. Because, well, you've got

> the, the robots and the like and the transfer lines, where the product... um...is put in by a machine or some worker and comes out as a finished product at the end of the line, you know. Well, that's a major difference. But let me tell you, among the workers, nowadays, there's no communication any more, there is no breathing space any more. It is much more stressful today, because you must always be mentally alert; in the past, it was like this, we also worked two or three shifts on occasion. (...) But at that time, during late shift or night shift, you had a break at least three or four hours before the end of work. During this break, you would sit together and have a chat with your colleagues. About topics, such as family or children. About everything, about all the world and your wife. But this is not possible anymore. People are supposed to be on location punctual to the minute. And to stop working to the minute. There is no communication anymore. I think this is sad, and the stress, well, that they...um... when people age, I'm talking of the production and so on, you know. I'd say it's almost the same for salaried employees. They are even monitored on the computer, how many strokes they do and how long their computer has been running and so on. It's not so easy, you know.

In the interviews, the older employees repeatedly compared today's work situation, where there is "no breathing space" for the individual, with the work experience of the past. In their view, the changes have brought a general increase in the workload, which manifests itself in a quickened work pace and a loss of breathing space at work. This is described by a former worker as follows:

> It was quieter (...) at work, not so hectic. Yes. You finished one task and then you did the next. Nowadays, you do three tasks at the same time. When you are doing one thing, you think of something else to do, wait a minute, I just finish this quickly, because of that. How hectic nowadays! This hectic. Well, you were more of a quiet type at that time.

In the view of the older interviewees, these changes, which appear to affect workers as well as salaried employees, have a negative impact on the social relations between the employees and lead to a general increase of psychological stress due to the work situation.

> Well, you had to do more physical work, but you still had more breathing space. Today, the stress is more of a psychological nature. And people, how they cope. It's not so easy. They really have their difficulties. It's not so easy.

However, the increased workload and the extended control were not the only consequences of the restructuring processes specified by the interviewees. In the view of the older interviewees, the social cohesion within the companies was stronger in the past. This is not only reflected in the comments above about the family feeling within the company but is also evident from their descriptions of a considerable internal solidarity of the workforce in the face of plant closures. It is noticeable that the older interviewees tended to have a negative view of today's social relations. Not only did they point out an increasing social isolation, which was partially attributed to the intensified use of computers by young people, but they also observed a growing competition and erosion of solidarity in today's society. An interviewee who was born in 1931 talked about his last years at work:

> It became worse in later years, when bullying appeared at work. When people competed against each other for work positions. By way of backstabbing, right? And a "see how great I am" attitude towards superiors.

When comparing the statements of older interviewees with those of younger interviewees, a different perspective on today's work situation and social relations can easily be identified. While younger workers based their narratives on their experiences within the last few years, older workers compared the current situation with experiences from over their whole working lives and therefore arrived at different views to those of the younger workers. Although the speed of the conveyor belts might have increased, the social life of a 31-year-old MAN worker, for instance, is still very much shaped by his social contact with his fellow workers even today – so much so that it induced him to move from Nuremberg to Fürth in order to create some distance. He recounted the following:

> Somehow you also need a certain amount of privacy. Well, I noticed in Nuremberg, and we later moved away from there, that no matter where we went, there was always some MAN colleague waiting, who had something he wanted from you. Or the other way round, you wanted something from him. Or you had a conversation with them. But always about work. And now my brother works at MAN too. So if we two are sitting together, our conversations are all about work too. (...) In this respect, it was for the better that we moved to Fürth. Because there are not so many MAN people at that place.

A former foundry mechanic who was born in 1972 also talked about his good working relations:

> Well, there are certainly work colleagues who have become real friends. And then, there are those work colleagues you visit about once in a week, or sometimes meet outside work. Or you know that a work colleague has something you can borrow. Some work colleagues call on me and say, you got a trailer don't you? Or you got the big car jack, well, and then, there are a lot of work colleagues you just see at work.

However, the interviewee also related different experiences and pointed out that his earlier employment at an agency for temporary work did not provide him with an opportunity to form any close relationships:

> At the temp agency, things were a bit more anonymous. Because your colleagues at work changed continually. You would also meet once in a while, but there was not enough time to form a committed relationship.

One industrial clerk, who was born in 1980, thought of her workplace today as a family-like environment similar to the older workers' account of the workplaces of the past. She said the following:

> We get along very well. (...) This is really what you would wish for, such a nice...um...familial atmosphere. (...) I just think that these relations between people are enormously important at work. After all, you actually spend most of the day at work. (...) We are so open with each other. And with others. That's such a good thing. (...) And we almost always go out to lunch together.

Unlike the older industrial workers, who lamented the loss of breathing space in connection with the changes at their work place, the young office clerk found some room for social exchange during work hours.

> It also happens on occasion that three or four of us talk for an hour or so about our private life during working hours. But nobody gets told off for this. And I think this is OK, because you get back to work with new motivation.

However, the connotation has changed: the older workers consider it more of a rebellious activity to take some breathing space, an act of creating personal freedom and escaping the control at work. In contrast, the young office clerk describes the usage of breathing space as an opportunity to increase her work motivation and thus to boost her work performance as a whole.

Conclusion

Class has several dimensions that became visible in the workers' narratives: in addition to differences in economic capital, class relies on other elements as well. Even if such a conflict is implied only indirectly, class also sometimes appears to be a special interest of people that is contrasted with the different interests of their bosses. A common complaint about one's own powerlessness in work relations is an element of the workers' class. Other elements are the construction of oneself and others by specific habitus practices and with the fine differences in taste (Bourdieu 1984) but also the construction of oneself (as a practical person physically working with one's own body) and others by attributed cultural practices. However, one important issue that is visible in the workers' narratives needs more attention in the following chapter: the emotional expression of class through nostalgic narratives of past good times coming together with mourning, anger, a loss of acknowledgement of physical labour, the ruination of former work places and, in general, the social decline of workers.

Part II

Senses of place and transformed industrial landscapes

4 "Quite a shame"

Confrontations between workers nostalgia and optimistic official representations

In 2010, the head of Nuremberg's department for economic affairs claimed, in a statement tinged with optimism in the *Süddeutsche Zeitung* newspaper, that the city had moved "away from being a workers' city" towards "a city of academics" that provides new opportunities. The same year, Peter, an 81-year-old retired toolmaker, was less optimistic and told me that Nuremberg's transition towards becoming a service-providing city was "quite a shame."

This chapter is about the relationship between official representations of a transformed industrial urban landscape and the narrated and nostalgic memories of the workers who have actually experienced the transformation. Accordingly, two approaches to landscapes are incorporated here: the landscape as represented in texts and landscapes as personal memories. Against the backdrop of a post-industrial society that since the second half of the 1980s undergoes a transition from the production of goods to the provision of services, this book uses the example of the city of Nuremberg in North Bavaria to analyse how former manual workers whose physical skills are devalued cope with this transition, whereas theoretical forms of knowledge gain in value. Against the backdrop of metal workers' life narratives and official representations of Nuremberg, this chapter examines the differences and similarities between an optimistic official representation of a transformed post-industrial landscape full of new opportunities and the way retired workers remember it. It will be argued that both are elements of social knowledge in Nuremberg and specifically of a generation with a particular knowledge (Mannheim 1952 [1923]).

Based on the workers' narratives of their move up the social ladder as manual workers during Germany's golden age – the so-called *Wirtschaftswunder* (German for "economic miracle") – the aim here is to establish why those relatively well-off and socially secured retired manual workers (who have experienced a significant increase in purchasing power during their lifetime) find it difficult today to enjoy the social and economic effects of their social rise and feel nostalgic. This is answered by considering the workers' social class as relevant and implicit in their memories and everyday practices (Savage 2000; Skeggs 2004; Reay 2005; Sayer 2005; Kirk and Wall 2011).

After discussing memories, social knowledge and landscape representations, this chapter analyses official representations of Nuremberg followed by the personal and identity-related memories of the people living and perceiving the landscapes represented in official representations. Those representations were not selected with a focus on history but on such representations of the past that were publicised in a prominent way. This is reflected, for example, in the 2004 front cover of an exhibition catalogue (and the exhibition poster) by the city archive on the history of South Nuremberg and the current exhibition in the industrial museum. Those present-day representations of the past are related to prominent recent representations of today such as, for example, on the city's official website or by leading politicians in interviews.

Official representations and personal memories of urban landscapes as social knowledge

Life narratives are a public presentation of the self. Therefore, the official representations of Nuremberg in images, heritage and political statements and the narrated presentation of interviewees share similarities. Both talk to a public and include selected elements or views in their narrations.

Official representations of transformed landscapes such as in city advertisements (Kearns and Philo 1993; Paddison 1993; Bradley, Hall and Harrison 2002) and city branding (Vanolo 2008), monuments and museums (Frank 2016), statements by politicians or photographs in the media (Millington 2013) are powerful elements in recent urban politics geared towards the creation of an entrepreneurial city that aims to attract investors, tourists and new middle classes while working against the needs of lower classes (Harvey 1990; Hubbard and Hall 1998). Overall, this strand of research has not paid any specific attention to the people working or residing within the transformed landscapes; an exception is a quantitative survey by Zhang and Zhao (2009) that demonstrated differences between the official branding of Beijing and the way the people see Beijing.

Analyses that consider both official representations and personal experiences do so mainly from a perspective that sets powerful representations into contrast with powerless, nostalgic people (as in studies on gentrification or urban-branding strategies). Scant research has been conducted on the relationship between memories of people who have experienced transformations of urban landscapes and those official representations. This chapter analyses this relationship by considering both as elements of social knowledge in terms of: "what people 'know' as 'reality' in their everyday, non- or pre-theoretical lives. (…) It is precisely this 'knowledge' that constitutes the fabric of meanings without which no society could exist" (Berger and Luckmann 1966: 27).

People's memories do not exist outside a general social knowledge and can be framed within the concept of a collective social memory (Halbwachs

1992 [1941]). That social memory is stored in urban landscapes and places is widely acknowledged (Hayden 1995; Johnson 2003; Degnen 2005; Meusburger, Heffernan and Wunder 2011). In this chapter, it is South Nuremberg that is the storehouse of memories expressed in the interviewee's life narratives.

As demonstrated in Chapter 1 memories are linked to landscape and places mainly in two aspects. First, this refers to those officially produced heritage landscapes of memories, the "lieux de mémoire" (Nora 1989) or the "memoryscapes" that represent "a history of power through which specific memories have been materialised in the urban landscapes" (Edensor 2005a: 131) and which are important for a collective memory (Hoelscher and Alderman 2004). The second aspect refers to that of the "milieu de mémoire" (Nora 1989) or of "living memories" (Mah 2010) that are related to former personal experiences of the people who memorise the mundaneness of everyday landscapes (Jones 2005; Espinoza, Piper and Fernández 2014; Wheeler 2014). Karen Till calls for memory studies to be sensitive to how individuals and social groups make sense of the past through their relationship with places and "suggest[s] that places become a part of us, even when held in common, through the intimate relationships individuals and groups have with them" (Till 2008: 108). This has been demonstrated by academic work on memories of transformed places in a self-reflexive way (Davidson 2009: Jones and Garde-Hansen 2012), for example, with an analysis of the relation between decayed materiality and memories (Edensor 2005b; DeSilvey 2012). This perspective has been influenced by Walter Benjamin's concept of the flâneur (Benjamin 2006 [1938]) that embodied individual and collective memories and experiences with dominant processes, cultural traditions and meanings (Gilloch 1996; Frisby 2007).

A different perspective is taken when analysing the narrated memories and experiences in transformed places of common people by paying attention to the relevance of class (Blokland 2001; Rogaly and Taylor 2009; Mah 2012; Taylor 2012; Meier and Aytekin 2019). People's narrated memories are linked to class, because class refers also to specific experiences and a common knowledge based on the class position in social hierarchy (Bourdieu 1984). These are linked to shared memories and collective identifications as associated with the industrial past of a region (Mah 2012: 52). Such a sense of belonging to a class is frequently associated with a sense of belonging to places and shared emotions (Reay 2005). Transformations of those places as a result of the closure of steelworks, for example, can hence generate painful emotions of loss (Walkerdine 2010). Class-related memories are based not only on those experiences in places and landscapes but also on "a container of stories about the past" (Blokland 2001: 272) that are included in the collective knowledge of a specific group. This chapter refers to such intimate relationships with places expressed in the life memories of people and relates them to official representations which are like memory sites subject to contestations and power struggles.

Personal memories and official representations are intertwined as they refer to and produce a common social knowledge. Both are realised in a specific socioeconomic context and period. They are related as people's memories are told against the background of a specific socioeconomic context that also leaves an imprint on official representations.

From a "workers' city" to a "city of academics": transformed representations of Nuremberg

As one of the main economic centres in Germany, Nuremberg today has both significant manufacturing and service sectors with particular strengths in engineering, communication technology, manufacturing systems and services sectors such as insurance and research (see Chapter 2). During 19th-century industrialisation, Nuremberg held a prominent position exemplified by Germany's first railway line linking Nuremberg and the nearby city of Fürth and the rapid expansion of craft and industry beyond the old borders of the city. South Nuremberg developed into the major industrial district of Nuremberg from the second half of the 19th century. The way the past of Nuremberg's south is represented today is exemplified by a picture postcard that was published on the occasion of the meeting of

Figure 4.1 Postcard from 1899 for the meeting of the Society of Engineers in Nuremberg on the front cover of the exhibition catalogue (Beer 2004), Stadtarchiv Nürnberg, Av 8774.8° (15).

the Society of Engineers in 1899 and has been republished recently by the city archive as a poster for an exhibition on the history of South Nuremberg and subsequently featured on the cover of the exhibition catalogue (Beer 2004) (Figure 4.1).

The postcard presents South Nuremberg as a single industrial plant reaching as far as the city centre and Nuremberg Castle. The whole city seems to be characterised by and dependent on this prosperous district with its smoking chimneys and large industrial plants. Also remarkable is the man at the front of the picture holding a large sledgehammer. He obviously looks strong enough to be able to use the hammer, anvil or tongs and is standing in a self-confident pose – due presumably to his ability to cope with hard work – in front of the industrial plants. The postcard portrays Nuremberg as an industrial city made up of tough and proud men working in industry. Foucault demonstrated that bodies are historical constructs and are disciplined and regulated by multiple techniques and disciplinarians (Foucault 1979 [1976]). The body in the standardised Taylorist industrial production is an example par excellence for being regulated by a tight regime of industrial work (Braverman 1974). This demand for a suitable masculine body able to work with the materiality of tools and machines in the industrial South Nuremberg is represented on this postcard.

Representations of urban districts and cities can change over time (Eade 1997). Having been the "red city of workers" with South Nuremberg as its powerhouse, Nuremberg during the Nazi era was presented as the City of the Nazi Party Rallies held in South Nuremberg. After the end of the Nazi regime, large parts of Nuremberg destroyed by bombing were reconstructed. But it was not until the 1980s that South Nuremberg was portrayed mainly as a residential district of the working class. After several factory closures since the 1970s, which saw the dominant metalworking and electrical sectors lose around 50,000 workers, South Nuremberg today is widely considered as a problematic district characterised by a relatively high unemployment rate, a high poverty rate and a high proportion of low-qualified and poorly integrated people with a migrant background. In 2000, the weekly journal *Der Spiegel* described South Nuremberg as an urban district marked by social problems, deprivation and criminality (Der Spiegel 2000: 114ff.).

The image of a socially deprived urban district was an issue the city government wanted to resolve. Besides other transformations, also the representation of this district changed. Now South Nuremberg is depicted in a different way: in 2008, for example, the local newspaper *Südstern* described South Nuremberg as being "fit for the future, trendy and multicultural." In general, the development of South Nuremberg is portrayed positively by the press and by politicians (Klumpp-Leonard 2007; Stadt Nürnberg 2007). The previous representation of South Nuremberg has evolved from a district with problems to a dynamic quarter of opportunities. It is an impression backed by city district festivals such as the Südstadtfest or the Spirit of Asia festival. In general, the local government has tried hard to change Nuremberg's image of a predominantly working-class city. Mayor Ulrich

Maly said that Nuremberg today is no longer an industrial city, but a city where industry is important and, as already mentioned at the beginning of this chapter, the head of the city's department for economic affairs said that Nuremberg had turned "away from being a workers' city" to become "a city of academics" (Süddeutsche Zeitung 2011). This changed representation of Nuremberg is also reflected by the city's official website (Stadt Nürnberg 2013). The economic section is titled "From an industrial city to the centre of the service sector" and features a photo of the Nuremberg skyline that underlines this representation. This view does not show an industrial factory area but rather a skyscraper – known as the Business Tower – of an insurance company (Nürnberger Versicherungsgruppe) that was completed in 2000 and is located in the east of the city.

The portrayal of Nuremberg and South Nuremberg has changed: even though Nuremberg Castle and the historic city remain at the forefront, they are now combined with the city's developed service sector or, as the city's marketing department puts it, the aim is a branding that shows "the contrast between the typical fried sausages and high-tech – thus between tradition and modernity" (Stadt Nürnberg 2009: 49). Industrial work carried out by hard-working manual labourers in factories does not feature in this representation, but rather a sophisticated service-sector infrastructure embodied by its icon, a high-tech skyscraper. It is a representation well-suited to what is considered a competition between cities for capital investment and for attracting the so-called creative class (Florida 2004; Florida 2005) of well-educated and mobile members of the middle class (Meier 2015). This interurban competition for attracting "talents" and investors is accomplished in general by promoting new economic developments, place marketing and rearranging the city's representation with reference to a post-industrial city of knowledge and innovation. Richard Florida's concept of the creative class was criticised for focussing on the lifestyles and presence of yuppies while overlooking the organisations and people not considered as creative in his work. This "has the effect of elevating creativity to the status of a new urban imperative – defining new sites, validating new strategies, placing new subjects and establishing new stakes in the realm of competitive interurban relations" (Peck 2005). The critique allows us to reflect on the shift in the representation of Nuremberg away from presenting strong manual labourers in an industrial setting towards a post-industrial landmark without the labourers but with the vision of creative human minds. It is not by chance that the image of the strong manual labourer is absent in recent representations of Nuremberg, as it does not fit in with the representational shift towards a "city of academics."

But industrial work is still present in Nuremberg, not only in factories but also in representations. Museums and monuments are important sites for such representations. It is marked as a specific characteristic of postmodernity that museum culture and the heritage industry have flourished since the late 1970s (Harvey 1990: 62). In Nuremberg, too, heritage and museums have boomed in the last few decades and heritage is localised in specific places

(Graham, Ashworth and Tunbridge 2000). Also previously Nuremberg was keen to boast heritage and museums as representing it as an important industrial city whose creativity was owed to a few men. This is highlighted by monuments like that of the founder of the Schuckertwerk (later merged with Siemens) Sigmund Schuckert, situated on the Schuckert Square in South Nuremberg or that of Anton von Rieppel the former chairman of the MAN (Figure 4.2).

Rather than showcasing strong working bodies from the industrial plants, it is the thinking body of the former capitalist that is displayed which fits in well with the representation of Nuremberg as a knowledge-based "city of academics." Men like Theodor von Cramer-Klett (1817–1884) or Sigmund Schuckert (1846–1893) who are credited with being the creative founders

Figure 4.2 Memorial of Anton von Rieppel on the Volckamerplatz (photo taken by Lars Meier).

responsible for the economic success of large industrial plants – but who also took responsibility for the workers (as a “good patriarch”) – have been honoured by monuments that still exist today or by pubs (e.g. the closed “Zum Vater Schuckert” or “Zum Schuckertsheim”), squares or streets (e.g. “Schuckertstraße”) named after them since around 1900 (Beer 2004: 193). It was also in 1899 that Germany’s first railway museum was opened in Nuremberg. This museum heavily features Germany’s first railway line between Nuremberg and Fürth and is still open today. The representations of industrial history have a twofold focus on the performance of the male founder and on some outstanding technical products such as the first passenger train, the Adler – which is still an important element of the city’s marketing efforts (Figure 4.3) as a symbol of the region’s historical importance in industry and creativity – or that of a large diesel engine – built in 1908 and in operation until 1964 – still in place at the main entrance of the MAN plant.

But again, the people working in the plants who produced these technical products with their manual labour remain invisible in these representations. It is an invisibility that is occasionally combined with the visible highlighting of a former factory by means of a commemorative plaque or by preserving the outer shell of a former factory while transforming its use. This is the case

Figure 4.3 Advertisement of events around the 175th anniversary of the Adler in 2010 (photo taken by Lars Meier).

with the former Ofenwerk plant in the northeast of Nuremberg. Part of the company Riedhammer it is now being transformed into an exhibition hall for vintage cars. Here history comes back as a quotation (Zukin 2011). It is an illusion of a clean history lacking signs of manual working processes and of those who have worked there. Besides established monuments of male company founders, commemorative plaques or reconstructed industrial architecture, where the everyday life of the common people is absent, Nuremberg's industrial history is represented by new collections and museums that place a different focus on history as well. Especially the new Museum of Industrial Culture (Museum Industriekultur)[1] founded in 1988 which extended its exhibition area in 2000 promises: "Here work and everyday life become alive again" (Museum Industriekultur 2013a). Similar to the official representation, the Museum of Industrial Culture also contextualised the exhibition as the history of manual industrial work in Nuremberg. This becomes evident on the museum's website, which states that by going through the exhibition along the so-called *Museumsstrasse* chronicling the 200 years of industrial development in Nuremberg, visitors witness "the development of Nuremberg from an industrial city to a stronghold of the service sector, science, research and education" (Museum Industriekultur 2013b).

The museum aims to integrate the history of technology with social history by displaying places from everyday life like a pub, a bicycle shop (Figure 4.4) and a classroom as well as some selected machines and equipment. Instead of ignoring the everyday life of the common people, the museum puts it at the centre of attention. Inside the museum, history is simulated (Jameson 1992) through artificially constructed patina and integrated historical fragments, which are the main elements of the exhibitions, as well as individual narratives on former living conditions.

It has been argued that the specific kinds of representation turn history into a contemporary creation that is a costume drama (Hewison 1987). This kind of heritage creates an illusion of authentic history that can also be taken for real history and is therefore considered to have an impact on personal memories and social knowledge. The complexity of everyday life is reduced in interesting ways. The bodily exertion and the physical dangers are more or less invisible. Also social conflicts within the workplace and everyday life or power relations between collectives and classes are rarely shown directly here or in similar exhibitions (Dicks 2008). Instead, there tends to be a nostalgic representation of history that hides the negative consequences of industrial production or social conflicts. It is a representation that stands in contrast to the personal experiences of the workers, such as in social conflicts or physical toll on the body. For example, Peter,[2] an 81-year-old toolmaker who worked for decades for the manufacturing company MAN, offers a rather contrasting image:

> There I saw how women lost their fingers [because of the presses]. The presses, they had tons of presses. They were so loud, the firm was located on Gostenhofer Hauptstrasse, that you could hear them, bang, even at Plärrer. (...) Actually, these were different times.

Figure 4.4 Reconstructed bicycle shop in the Museum Industriekultur (photo taken by Lars Meier).

A 72-year-old former lathe operator, Max, who worked for Grundig, remembers:

> I had an accident in 1969. My finger got caught in an injection-moulding machine and was bruised.

The workers remember their bodies being exposed to dangerous experiences, suffering physical injury and being aware of their physical skills that enabled them to do manual work. But those experiences are not widely referred to in heritage or other official representations of Nuremberg. Instead of representing manual work based on physical ability, manual industrial labour is now depicted as history of Nuremberg. Social knowledge is represented and changed representations reflect the transformation in social knowledge. Workers' memories of their own working experiences do not fit in well with these representations, but as shown in the following section, the workers themselves are nostalgically aware of the shift of representation that is also a devaluation of strong working bodies and the workers' class.

Workers' nostalgia – class and a shift of social knowledge

Social knowledge is embedded in different sources and expressed by different kinds of organisations, practices and texts (Berger and Luckmann 1966). Therefore, it comes as no surprise that there are also similarities between the official representation of Nuremberg and the memories of former workers. This is because both are expressions and elements of a common social knowledge. The former manual workers portray Nuremberg and South Nuremberg as a city of transformation. It is a transformation where industrial work is considered to be declining, whereas unemployment and employment in the service sector are believed to be on the rise. Werner, a 71-year-old metal worker, said:

> We have lived in Nuremberg for around 40 years. How Nuremberg has changed. One has to look back at what was there and what was not there in the past. (…) Some urban districts have changed completely. (…) Or the huge tower of the Nuremberg insurance company. It is the landmark, yes.

It is also the transformation of the overall representation of the city away from a proud industrial culture towards a representation of a service-sector city – vividly expressed with the "landmark" of the Nuremberg insurance company – that is of some emotional relevance for industrial workers in older age. Peter had the following to say about a conversion from an industrial city to a service-sector city:

> Looking back, what really upsets me is that once there were so many people employed, and that there are so few left today. Er, actually for all of Nuremberg that was an industrial town after all. That is where things were manufactured, where parts were made, and all of a sudden, all that has turned into a service-providing city. Well this is really quite a shame.

The transformed representations towards a post-industrial city match the workers' narratives of the current situation. However, what differs is that while official representations depict this as a positive development of opportunity, the workers' memories are imbued with nostalgia. According to them, the conversion of the former industrial city into today's service-based city is "quite a shame."

Industrial workers' nostalgic memories and the filtering out of unpleasant memories in an idealised "golden past" (Williams 1973; Davis 1979;

Atia and Davies 2010) within transformed industrial landscapes (Chapter 5; Kirk, 2007; Strangleman 2007) and communities (Chapters 7 and 8; Revilla, Jefferys and Tovar 2013; Charlesworth 2000) have been widely discussed. But the source of nostalgia is vague for the relatively well-off population of retired industrial workers who have personally experienced Germany's economic boom since the 1950s. This is also obvious in their narratives of personal success accompanied by rising incomes, a considerable increase in consumption possibilities and practices (food, cars, holidays, etc.), better working and living conditions and generous pensions.

In general there is a "tendency to homogenise collective memory and thus to underestimate the extent to which collective memory can be a container for a diversity of colliding and fragmented meanings of the past" (Conway 2010: 444). But memories like nostalgic memories are cultural practices that depend "on where the speaker stands in the landscape of the present" (Stewart 1988: 227) and social groups of people might have different collective memories (Halbwachs 1992 [1941]). Nostalgia is more than a conservative and idealised viewpoint of a harmonic past (Strangleman 2007; Strangleman 2014). It is also an expression of a specific form of an emotionally featured memory in the present that is a manifestation of class identity and provides information about the social position today.

People's memories have a selective and identity-related quality and it is also class that is of relevance here. "Class is sometimes the unstated absent presence" (Woodward et al. 2014: 427), but the relevance of class with regard to access to economic and social resources has been demonstrated (Sayer 2005) and also class-related emotions (Reay 2005) and cultural practices can be seen (Bourdieu 1984; Adams and Raisborough 2008; Le Roux et al. 2008). Class is also a source of identification with a social group (Reid 1998; Skeggs 2004; Kirk 2007) apparent in Peter's narrative and his complaint "that there were once so many people employed and that there are so few left today" which demonstrates his identification with those workers. For him it is "a shame" that the former industry city is now a service city. He considered industrial work to be "where things were manufactured, where parts were made" in contrast to what is produced in the service sector. This refers to a general contrast between manual labour and work in the service sector. The interviewees frequently described themselves as being able to work with their hands and being practically minded and contrasted this with the intellectual work. Using the example of a worker's life in a transformed industrial town, Simon Charlesworth demonstrated that workers' habitus, which once carried cultural capital, became dislocated and devaluated (Charlesworth 2000). The workers' habitus of being physically practical and capable of producing "things," as Peter put it, no longer fits in well with the service "city of academics" as shown in the official representations. Their class-based knowledge of being practical and their former work stand in stark contrast to the official representation and are devaluated within the represented new "city of academics."

Many workers are still proud of their physical working skills and told me a great deal about their abilities in handicrafts and wood and metal work. The results of their labour can be seen in various manufactured items found in their apartments. For instance, Lutz, a former fitter born in 1945 said:

> I'm glad that I was forced to train as a fitter. Because I have become very creative, I work a lot. And I have learned a lot, indeed. And I'm skilful in handicrafts. I do a lot of metal work, a lot of woodwork. Cases, for instance. Such things I assemble by myself from leftover materials. These are the leftover materials from the case. This is a Vogelauer parlor [Vogelauer: furniture producer]. I copied it and made a cover for the case from it. This is all in my head, I do everything myself.

Max, a former motor mechanic born in 1952, expressed his pride of doing physical labour in the following narrative by describing the renovation work on his house to me as follows:

> For instance, I just bought the windows, but installed them myself, being a craftsman, until, well, until 2007, 2008 I still installed all the plates myself, altogether 3.6 tons. Well, I even bought a mortar mixer just to prepare the mortar. And so on, yes. Then I did shovel work at the front and at the back of the house and I re-insulated the foundation. I did all that on my own. Well, for I'm a lone fighter, you know.

But the results of such work and the ability to "do" are now only private and no longer valued within official representations of Nuremberg. Peter and Lutz were part of the industrial city with their identity as workers and with their knowledge-based abilities based on a trained body. Even if industrial production is still going on in Nuremberg, such physical skills are absent in the representations of the city. Transformations of urban landscapes, work and community are one of the main focus areas of the biographic interviews. The older interviewees especially complained about the transformations that are mostly considered as a loss. It seems that as a former worker in a so-represented former industrial city that has transformed into a post-industrial city, the knowledge learnt in the former time of the industrial city embedded in the habitus has lost its relevance.

In a seminal text, Karl Mannheim argued that generations differ not only by date of birth but by common experiences typical for their generation in the wake of specific historical events (Mannheim 1952 [1923]). Williams also insisted that the structure of feeling, as the relevance of social forces for the shape of affective lives, is the culture of a period and that "no generation speaks quite the same language as its predecessors" (Williams 1977: 131).

Especially workers with a long family tradition of living and working in Nuremberg refer to a knowledge of the industrial city that overlaps families and generations and relate this to the current situation. With such a class-based knowledge from a former time, also younger people feel very old. 44-year-old Melanie, who grew up in South Nuremberg as the child of industrial workers, said the following about the transformation:

> Some buildings are like they were before. But it is all so dynamic, for me changes are taking place so quickly. I cannot keep pace with that. Then you say to yourself, well was there something different or not? That is sometimes a bit difficult for me. Also for me and I am not that old. But then I feel that I am very old. If you remember the former times, then I think I am 60 years old or so.

Melanie sees the ongoing transformation in South Nuremberg as a difficult challenge. She feels unfit to keep up with the dynamics of social acceleration (Rosa 2013). She does not have the suitable knowledge that might help her to deal with the new situation. She continued by telling me about the consequences of the transformations on her everyday life, which is the story of losing the suitable knowledge. She said:

> Many of the old pubs I'd known for a long time and that were really cosy have gone; this is a pity. (…) For example, the "Rumpelkammer" which I liked very much. It had sofas and it was really cosy, but it is not there anymore. I went there sometimes with my ex-husband. And there was also the "Mania", a hard-rock pub, which was great; it had loud music and good music. But it is closed now. (…) That is sad, because for my generation there is nothing left of interest. And if you look at the rapid changes to the shops. One shop opens and one shop closes. It's all so fast. In former times you knew, okay here is this shop and there is that shop. You could say, okay lets go to Horten [shopping centre] or to Woolworth or how was it called? I'm not sure; it was named Kaufhalle for some time and then Woolworth and then again different and now I think it is again Kaufhalle, as far as I know. (…) And also the Atrium cinema has closed. When I was young, we went there for the children's show on Sundays. That was nice; it was cheap and it was our cinema.

The respondents frequently associate the transformations of the city infrastructure, buildings and shops with the loss of their former communities. For Melanie, the closing of the cinema is also an event that embodies the disintegration of her former community. In contrast to the official representation where dynamic development is presented as a potential, the interviewed former workers experience it rather as uncertainty. This feeling is also voiced by an 81-year-old man who told me that the transformations in South Nuremberg would push out the poor. He said: "the residential areas will be transformed to become more attractive and those with cheap apartments will be pushed out." Other interviewees see the transformations that are taking place in a different way – not as a process of gentrification but with a feeling of uncertainty as a process of rising violence and disintegration. Irene, a 60-year-old former warehouse clerk, who worked for decades for the company AEG, said:

> I don't like South Nuremberg, I don't like the noise and I don't like the cultural differences there. (…) It has not transformed in a positive way. In former times it was more quiet. Around Kaufhof now you cannot go into the underground because there are terrible people there, very aggressive. I don't see anything positive in South Nuremberg today.

The older manual workers do not consider South Nuremberg as a district of opportunity, unlike the official representations. For them it is rather a district of challenges where one's habitus and knowledge has become outdated and belittled as no longer fitting in with the "city of academics."

Conclusion

The city is trying hard to change the representation of Nuremberg from a "workers' city" towards a "city of academics." Even if there is still industrial work going on in Nuremberg, the official representation of the city has shifted the focus on presenting Nuremberg as a city where industrial work is more a part of its history while showcasing the city today as a hub of the knowledge-based service sector. Industrial work based on physical activity is mainly presented as an experience of former times.

It became apparent that general transformations find expression in adjusted personal narratives and memories. This chapter demonstrated that an optimistic representation of a transformed industrial landscape towards a landscape of academics leaves an imprint on the workers. The shift in representation towards Nuremberg being a "city of academics" is an offence to the worker's class identity. This is expressed by the workers' nostalgic memories. Because nostalgia is a cultural practice, "it depends on where the speaker stands in the landscape of the present" (Stewart 1988: 227). This chapter has not demonstrated the relevance of class in terms of the importance of the economic status of the former skilled workers whose biographical life stories tell of a rise in social standing. Class identity as manual workers is important as a source of emotions and of a sense of being suitable and valued for one's physical abilities and practical skills. The workers have a knowledge-based intimate relationship with the industrial landscape, and the industrial landscape has become a part of them and of their class identity as manual workers. Their nostalgia of a better past, even with its lower wages and lower economic status, is grounded in a transformed social knowledge. The social knowledge of former times, when manual physical labour was relevant, has lost its value and does not fit in with the present. The official representation of new landscapes for the talented middle class confirms that manual work and its knowledge are no longer valued, while the knowledge of the so-called creative class is appreciated. The former workers address the transformed representation of Nuremberg in their narratives. They have to cope with their feelings with regard to having knowledge that is no longer needed. The workers try hard to defend their knowledge by arguing against the expertise of the creative class or they present themselves as being eager to learn and accumulate new knowledge by adapting to the transformed Nuremberg.

Notes

1 The "Museum Industriekultur" is located in the East of Nuremberg and situated in the remains of the former screw factory that was part of a former ironwork plant – the "Eisenwerk Tafel" established in 1876 and which closed down in 1975.
2 To secure the interviewees' anonymity all names are pseudonyms.

5 Class-related senses of place and frightening encounters with haunted workplaces

On 22 September 2002, in the Maxhütte in Sulzbach-Rosenberg[1] (see Chapter 2), approximately 800 workers poured hot liquid steel into the blast furnace and took the cooled product to the rolling mill for the last time. Following the shutdown of the Maxhütte,[2] the last steel works with a blast furnace in Bavaria Germany, most of the rolling mill was scrapped, and the casting machine sold to China. Today there is little left of the Maxhütte. Just a large – and contaminated – slag heap, gutted buildings and the remains of the blast furnace on a 60-hectare industrial area. But even though nearly everything to do with the former steel work is gone, former workers sometimes climb a nearby hill called the Schlossberg, for another look at what was once their workplace (Figure 5.1).

Sixty-six-year-old Karl who worked as an engine driver for 26 years at the Maxhütte describes a regular occurrence at the Schlossberg:

> People arrive at six o'clock in the morning – as if the blast-furnace was still there. Many come every day to the Maxhütte, just to look. And these are often people who are already getting their pension. What a picture of misery. Yes it is a picture of misery. The closure of the steelworks was the kind of life event that you never forget. It's different if a company doesn't have any particular importance for you. If you can say "well, I was just a number in the company". Then that's okay for you. But this was my company, and that's what everybody who worked there said about it. "It was my company."
>
> (Karl, 66 years, former engine driver)

Industrial ruins are metaphors of transition and change (Pusca 2010), as well as material structures that were, in former times, suitable to a specific regime of accumulation (Harvey 1990; Mitchell 1998) as "an inevitable result of capitalist development" (Edensor 2005a: 4). Sites and ruins transformed by time hold information about change in political-economic and social structures. The focus of this chapter is on the memories of those who have experienced such transformations within their working life.

As Karl remembers in the sequence above, transformed workplaces continue to attract former workers and awaken strong emotions. The

Figure 5.1 The Maxhütte seen from the Schlossberg (photo taken by Lars Meier).

ex-workers, now pensioned, are drawn to their former workplaces, even if those places are now in a different shape, and have lost their former purpose. In the former workers' memories, that which is absent today is reincarnated in a haunting sense. What form this takes, however, depends on who is remembering.

As with studies on the politics of memory, which focus on official memory sites, this chapter examines the subject from a new angle. Those studies contain powerful official representations of landscapes as texts (DeLyser 2003), containing interviews, for example, with owners of memory sites (Maddern 2008), the way in which these sites are represented in museums, and heritage structures under scrutiny (DeLyser 1999). Because the Maxhütte is also an official memory site, it could be considered as a subject for this kind of research. There is an ongoing public debate about which industrial monuments and icons of a former industrial age should be saved from these ruins, for tourism purposes. In the nearby town of Sulzbach-Rosenberg there is a museum which tells the history of the Maxhütte. The slag heap has been refurbished for possible tourism use, and the area is sometimes used for a 24-hour-long mountain bike race – a world cup event.

But this is not what attracts former workers. They visit the Maxhütte because of their personal memories of the time they worked there. For them, the Maxhütte is a personal memory site. That which is missing in their lives today looms hauntingly in their memories of former times. These memories, which may well be emotional experiences, are triggered by an encounter with a former place of work, and by narrating lengthy descriptions of these former times in the context of a life story interview situation.

Visiting the ruin of Maxhütte today or viewing it from a nearby hill gives rise to vivid memories and strong emotions for ex-employees. In this chapter, people who worked at a particular place for a long time describe their recollections from those locations. Their memories of the place as it was and the realisation of how it is now can be a highly emotional experience. They frequently own souvenirs which they display in their living rooms, such as a photograph of the factory (Figure 5.2). These artefacts bear witness to a deep emotional connection with their former place of work.

Industrial ruins and transformed industrial plants that were relevant in the workers' biographical narratives are discussed. Most of these sites are located directly in Nuremberg (like AEG, MAN and Grundig) or – as in the case of Maxhütte – are nearby and are visited by interviewees currently living in Nuremberg (see Chapter 2). By analysing the workers' place-related emotions, the distinction between a set of objective conditions which define class, the experience of being employed as a worker, and the subjective

Figure 5.2 Photo of the MAN factory on an apartment wall (photo taken by Lars Meier).

consciousness of one's own class position, is investigated. This chapter demonstrates the political aspect of supposedly very personal cultural characteristics within emotions and experiences.

Absence and haunting of former times in biographic narrations

Absence is a relative concept with a temporal dimension. What is absent today is absent from an identity-related perspective, which is fed by the specific experiences of the workers interviewed. This historical dimension is expressed in the memories within the life story interviews. It is within the context of these biographical interviews that a place is considered, not only in its actual representation but also as a former experience. In the workers' memories, absence is created by the relationship between what is encountered today and what is remembered from former experiences at the place of work, before the transformation occurred. The workers' sense of place and the emotions connected to their former workplace are especially strong during narrations of an imagined encounter, suggested by the interviewer, with the former workplace as it is today.

The formerly present structures which are now absent, come alive in these memories – as hauntings, which are, in effect, present absences. The metaphor of spectral haunting has featured prominently since the end of the 1990s (Bell 1997; Hetherington and Degen 2001; Wylie 2007; Maddern and Adey 2008; Davidson 2009; Coddingtona 2011) with references to the work of Derrida (1994). Against the background that the present exists only with respect to the past, he has developed the metaphor of haunting as something which folds time and unsettles the linear sense of time as it is represented. A haunting evokes a sense of injustice and triggers emotion. A haunting brings the past into the present, because what was there is remembered and given a relationship to the present by the ex-workers. As Gordon puts it:

> haunting is a very particular way of knowing what has happened or is happening. Being haunted draws us effectively, sometimes against our will and always a bit magically, into the structure of feeling of a reality we come to experience, not as cold knowledge, but as transformative recognition.
>
> (Gordon 2008: 8)

Broader transformations and their impact on the individual life can be seen from this metaphor. Because haunting is "a process that links an institution and an individual, a social structure and a subject, a history and a biography" (Gordon 2008: 19). By referring to haunting, that which the workers have lost in the past becomes palpable here. Using this metaphor, the past becomes what is experienced and seen by the workers today. The haunting appears in conjunction with the workers visiting their former work places and it involuntarily creeps into their biographic interviews. It wells up inside their narratives and during encounters with the site – without them wanting this to happen in an explicit way. The haunting also has a repetitive character as it comes into being involuntary, again and again.

Since this chapter is on haunting as perceived by those with former experiences of these places, it differs from the perspective of considering a ghost as a representation – or the traces of a representation of those who have gone long before, and who are now seen by others such as visitors to the site, or ghost hunters. In this chapter, the metaphor of haunting is considered from an identity specific perspective, with regard to the workers memories and experiences at their former places of work. The notion of haunting takes the workers back to times past. Today, from the top of the Schlossberg they see not only the remains of their former work place but also structures and events from the past. What, for others, is hidden under the layers of the current site, is visible for the former workers. A place contains traces of former times and its previous life, structures, atmospheres, people and experiences. But these traces cannot be seen by everyone. Only by those with experiences of the place. When encountering their workplaces today, the workers are haunted by former walls, machines or movements, which are seen and experienced exclusively by them. Those reliving their own experiences at their former place of work are haunted in such a way, proving that everyday geographies and identities are not without a past.

Class matters in an emotional geography, and in the context of a sense of place

Memories are not only an individual issue; the former manual workers come together at the Schlossberg to relate their memories and experience a shared sense of place as a class-related issue. This chapter demonstrates that those who worked at these now transformed places for a long period of time have a particular sense of place, related to class. Class is considered as a dynamic process here (see Chapter 1). This is because differences between classes are produced and reproduced through the daily practices and experiences of the individuals involved. It is this background of considering class in the context of daily practices and experiences, which allows class and place to come together in this chapter. This is not only because the work place was experienced by the workers on a daily basis, but also because the workers make their daily practices fit into the specific rules and structures of the workplace and its community.

The concept of a sense of place integrates an objective place and a subjective sense (Entrikin 1991; Tuan 2004). Using this concept, objective transformations of places and landscapes and individual responses to these transformed landscapes are seen in relation to each other. It is about whatever makes a place special for a person. Place-specific emotions are not only the result of objective qualities but also developed by the individual's subjective experiences there. From a phenomenological standpoint, immediate embodied experiences are integrated into the cultural rules and meanings which colour the way people behave, and how they perceive their surroundings (Merleau-Ponty 1962). Landscape from this perspective is a lifeworld, a milieu of engagement and of involvement. It is "a world to live in and not a scene to view" (Wylie 2007).

By putting its focus on the narrated experiences and emotions of former workers, this chapter is not on experience landscapes and absence with a phenomenological background, from a personal and emotional viewpoint by a subjective self-reflexive researcher (Jones 2005; Wylie 2009). Against such a background, one strand of research gives its attention to analysing the attraction of degradation and decay of cultural artefacts and ruins (Edensor 2005b; DeSilvey 2006).

The specific attraction of transformed or ruined places, for those who worked there before the transformation occurred, is considered in this chapter to be class-related. Memories and emotions are considered specific, as they are charged with being related to the social identity of class. From such a perspective, this chapter aims to fill the gap of a social identity-related emotional geography. Emotional geography (Bondi 2005; Davidson, Bondi and Smith 2005; Thien 2005; Pile 2010) is worked out mainly on the basis of personal identities and experiences. And when emotional geography is considered as a social identity-related issue, it is usually worked out using the example of gender identity (Valentine 1989; Anderson and Smith 2001; Bondi 2005; Collis 2005; Sharp 2009).

As demonstrated in Chapter 1, memory is not only central to self but is also a social activity. This is because it can be a collective matter, an expression and binding force of a social group identity (Hoelscher and Alderman 2004: 348). Biographic memories are therefore involved in the relationship between individual and social, as well as between past and present. Central elements within the biographic memories of the workers are related to family, relatives, work and home. These memories are spatially bound (Pile 2005) by places and landscapes, which are, in effect, "storehouses" of social and personal memories (Hayden 1995), and are bound up with processes of emotional attachment (Casey 1987; Jones 2005). For the workers, the strong emotional attachment to the workplace remains, even if it is transformed and they are of pensionable age. Bernd, a former Grundig worker, has such strong emotional attachments that he experiences them in his dreams (Figure 5.3):

> Lars: How do you feel when you drive past the Grundig site. What do you think?
> Bernd: There is still a feeling of coming home. (…) It's just that I liked it to be there. The worst thing is that I still dream of that time. (…) Of the work, really, I dream of the division. In my dreams I sometimes go in and can't ever find my way out. Or sometimes I drive in, and put my car in my parking spot, and when I want to go home I can't find my car. (both laughing) Totally crazy.
> Lars: That means you can't get away, then?
> Bernd: Yes (12)

> Lars: And what do you think it is that won't let you go?
> Bernd: I don't know. I don't know. The longing for home or (I: Yes) I don't know. (11) A few times I dreamt that I was going there – towards Grundig, Langwasser. But I can't find the way. It's very strange.

This emotional attachment to a place is made clear by an accompanying narration which articulates identity. The interviewees do not set their life narratives and experiences in a direct relationship to a class position. Their narratives are the constructions of individuality. It may be argued that this is because any inference of life style, behaviour or interests resulting from class membership, casts doubt on individuality. Class is in constant contradiction to a powerful social discourse that propagates individual freedom and self-fulfilment (Savage 2005).

The way in which we see and experience places is identity-related. People define themselves through places. The memories of ex-workers are connected to specific sites and communities – when their fellow workers occupied the landscape in question, for example. A sense of place, or a place identity is explained by psychologists as very personal – "a component of personal identity, a process by which, through interaction with places, people describe themselves in terms of belonging to a specific place" (Hernandez et al. 2007). But a sense of place is not entirely the result of individual experiences, emotions and meanings (Rose 1995). The workers' memories are not only an issue of a personal identity but also of their social class identity. Emotional relationships and feelings of affiliation to the work place develop over a long period of time (Altman and Low 1992), through everyday experiences at its

Figure 5.3 Former main entrance of the Grundig plant (photo taken by Lars Meier).

structure, rhythm and atmosphere and in a place-related worker community. A sense of place is an emotional link to a place, which has developed out of former experiences. Fleeting placements of moving material and people leave their mark in both the geography and the memory. By considering class identity by practices and experiences, the sense of place is seen here as one which is class-related. By recalling former encounters with other workers and consequently remembering the integration of self and the body into everyday work routines and rhythms at the workplace their class identity is indirectly reflected in their memories. It comes as no surprise that the place of work has a central role in the interviewees' biographic narratives, and is indirectly related to their identities as workers.

These encounters with former workplaces give rise to strong emotions in those who worked there. Their memories of the daily routines which took place there, as well as their past integration into a community, change their perception of the place. It becomes, for the interviewees, a home, and an "irreplaceable centre of significance" (Relph 1976: 39–40). Inclusion into a work place and its community brings about a shift in the individual's emotional relationship to it. The development of a class-related sense of place can be seen in the narrated memories of the workers. Gerda, a former warehouse clerk born in 1952, who worked for 36 years in the AEG plant in Nuremberg – closed in 2006 (Figure 5.4) – remembers a change in her personal perception, which is associated with the development of a sense of belonging to the work place.

Figure 5.4 The AEG sign that was highly visible on the top of the AEG main office building, now, after the closure, stands beside the building (photo taken by Lars Meier).

> When I was a child my parents and I frequently passed the AEG plant, and I would look at it and always think, "What an ugly building. I never want to work there." ... But time went by, and I did work at the plant and it didn't seem to be ugly anymore. (Laughs). And eventually, it became like a second family to me. For fifteen years, I looked forward to going to work. I would rather have let someone cut off my head than believe that the AEG plant would close. I never thought it would happen. It was a shock for me.
>
> (Gerda)

With the integration of the individual as a working person into a work place, the work process and the community, their emotional relationship to a place alters. For Gerda, the AEG plant was transformed from an ugly building to become "like a second family." Her inclusion as a worker, into the entire and rounded work process, made her feel like an integral part of the place, which then – for her, was not ugly anymore. This kind of close contact inevitably brings about a development of a sense of place, which, in turn, means that the worker's identity alters and becomes closely connected to the work place, its community and the work processes. With the closure of the factory, this inclusion as an integral part of the work place and its community is lost. But this does not leave feelings of emotional indifference towards the building once regarded as ugly. In the same way that Gerda's sense of place was once before dramatically changed by her integration into the plant that "became like a second family," the closure for her was a huge shock. And the emotions she experienced were similar to Karl's, described in the narration above as "this was my company, and that's what everybody who worked there said about it." Karl further describes his relationship to his former workplace when he explains that he never felt like "just a number."

These former workers consider their position as being much more than "just a number," in an industrial plant that was – and is – seen by them as "a second family" or as "my company." Within these interviews it becomes obvious that the workers did not see their positions in the workplace as a purely functional arrangement of capitalist labour. That labour is a commodity, and that the aim of the management and the owner of the plant was to accumulate capital out of gaining the surplus from their labour, doesn't feature in their view of their roles as workers within the former plant.

With the closure of the plant, the feelings of inclusion into the place and also the place-related identity is dramatically affected. As the plant – the "second family" or "my company," is closed, place bound integration into a working community – seen as a family structure – is dissolved. And when encountering the closed plant today, the former workers' belief that they were not just numbers and that the plant and its community was like their "second family" (Gerda), is shattered. In encountering what is left of the plant today, it becomes obvious to them that the work and production process they were included in, through their role and function as a worker, ultimately meant that each was in fact a number and part of a working body. The belief that each was a member of a "second family" is destroyed.

The encounter with the transformed or ruined work place today is a shock for them, because it is now clear that they were in the production process just workers who, unlike the owners of the plant, had no say in decisions on its development.

A nostalgic haunting of former good times and horrific emotions

Places and landscapes are the products of human activity and labour, and accordingly, are always in the process of becoming (Massey 1995; Mitchell 2003). Features such as materiality, atmosphere, rhythm and people may be altered and rearranged, but still their former structures have some resilience. And it is this durability of meaning and of materialities, which show the transformation of what was there before and is now absent. In heritage buildings and monuments, these traces are rearranged, as visible and powerful memory structures for the public (Kirshenblatt-Gimblett 1998; Till 2005; Frank 2016). But within these solid structures, there are also traces which are visible only to those who have specific memories of their own experiences at the corresponding place, and invisible to all others. These traces of former times can be fairly easily discerned, and are visible, for example, in a steel framework, as explained by Karl in the following interview excerpt.

> I visited the Maxhütte with some former colleagues; or rather I visited what is left of the Maxhütte today. It brought tears to my eyes, because now you can only see the steel framework. I said to myself: "This was my workplace, I worked there". The blast furnace was there, the roller mill was there, and and the steel mill was there. And now there are only naked steel frameworks. Nothing works anymore. For me this is … (he takes a deep breath) like looking at a dead person. I look from above the plant, from the Schlossberg, as it's called, directly down onto the Maxhütte. And I say, "no, it's not possible. Once eight or nine thousand people worked there – and now it's all over." (…) Today Sulzbach-Rosenberg is like a city of the dead. Before, there was life, there was action and and … now there is nothing. (…) And if you saw the people – sixty, sixty-five years old – crying like small children as the plant went down the drain. "My company is dying," they said. That was their Maxhütte.
>
> (Karl, 66 years, former engine driver)

When he looks at what is left of the Maxhütte, Karl perceives more than simply the visible traces, such as the "naked steel frameworks." His experiences as a worker at the Maxhütte have a keen influence on what he sees today. When he sees it from the Schlossberg his memories come alive. He looks at the material traces remaining, and he remembers that "there was life." His awakening memories while viewing the plant from the Schlossberg make his encounter with the Maxhütte an emotional experience. In Karl's narrative, he describes how his former workplace now appears as a "dead person" with "naked steel frameworks" where "nothing works anymore." The scene becomes filled with absences for Karl, as a result of seeing it in the context of remembered experiences from former times. If he encounters these "naked steel frameworks" today, Karl can see what is today not there for the others – but is still, because of his memories, there for him.

Karl remembers and sees, in his mind's eye, that "the blast furnace was there, the roller mill was there, and and the steel mill was there," and he cannot separate this knowledge from the scene in front of him. And when he encounters the Maxhütte today, Karl's perception of the area and his experiences there, are in effect, led by what is now absent for him but which still haunts him – making it for him, at any rate, still there. The former Maxhütte, its blast furnace, roller mill and steel mill are to Karl, spectres from the past, which continue to haunt him. Maddern and Adey write that "the figure of the ghost is often used as a means of apprehending that which we cannot explain, do not expect, understand, or struggle to represent" (Maddern and Adey 2008: 292). Karl also says that he "cannot believe this" and has no reasonable explanation of what has occurred. He says,

> It makes my heart ache. It's so hard to believe. I was there for 26 years, it was my company, and seeing it ruined like this, for no reason, is very hard for me to take in. Now it is like a dying giant.
>
> (Karl, 66 years, former engine driver)

The strong emotions evoked by encounters with former workplaces, now shut down or completely transformed, can be compared to a grieving process. Karl is expressing a feeling of shock combined with a denial of loss, in his explanation that his "heart aches" if he drives by the Maxhütte today. Other interviewees express great sorrow when they are confronted with their former workplaces – plants, such as Grundig, AEG or MAN, for instance. Lydia, a former worker in the closed Grundig plant in Nuremberg, describes how she feels when she drives past the former plant.

> Sometimes I start crying. I had some very good times there. Bad times too – but it was like my apartment – like my home. (…) It's where I grew up, right? That's where I grew up. I was 18 years old when I started work there [1984]. It's not easy. I'm really sorry that a well known company like that closed down. (…) I had a few colleagues, who actually became ill after the company closed down. Physically ill. Thirty years of work and then finished. Just like that. It's not easy.
>
> (Lydia)

When Gerda drives past the former AEG building today, she feels very emotional (Figure 5.5).

Figure 5.5 Former AEG building seen from the Fürther Strasse. This area is now used for various purposes (photo taken by Lars Meier).

> I look the other way (laughs). (…) Yes, with a sad glance, actually. Because a) it's not very often that I drive past it and b) because it still hurts when I think about it or when I see what happened to AEG. What they did to the company. They totally cut it into pieces, right? It's no longer the AEG company I know. So of course it hurts when I look at it.
>
> (Gerda)

For the members of the focus group, encountering the industrial area of the MAN is an emotionally demanding task. And driving past it automatically gives rise to strong feelings.

> Lars: "How do you feel when you drive by these buildings, which are being used so differently now?"
> Manfred: "Well, it hurts. It hurts, when you drive by them, when you've worked there a whole lifetime."
> Christian: "Yes, it definitely brings back memories."
> Manfred: "Of course." (…)

Ex-workers encountering their former workplace today find that it involves the energy sapping process of mourning a loss. Driving to his former workplace, Karl confronts his loss and considers what he remembers about it – and the haunts that are for him, still there. He says,

> Sometimes I find myself stopping by Sulzbach-Rosenberg. Then I go up to the Schlossberg and look down and I think: Hey, Karl, you worked there, in the shunting operation, then you drove there in a locomotive. You picked up the train there, and you fuelled the blast-furnace with coke, there. And now there is nothing left.
>
> (Karl, 66 years, former engine driver)

In confronting the Maxhütte, Karl imagines the routes he used to take, every day across the site. Karl remembers these movements as inextricably connected to the functioning of the entire industrial work and production process of the Maxhütte. But when he visits the Maxhütte, his memories aren't only of his own everyday working routines and movements. Because he sees his role as an integral part of the industrial area – which, in turn, was such a large part of the entire production process of, as Karl puts it "my company," he references that role as being a vital part of the whole work and production process in the Maxhütte.

Karl's routine body movements as an individual worker were part of an environment where such individual time-spaces and body routines commingled in a larger dynamic of interactions between several such individual time-space and body routines. David Seamon (1980) conceptualised this as place ballet[3] a process where communal exchanges and actions occur. Karl's memories are of his "body ballet" performance – his body moves and its time-space activities, fitting perfectly within the whole organisation of the work processes, as an integral part of a place ballet at the Maxhütte. Today, an encounter with the Maxhutte means that this "ballet" comes back to haunt Karl without his volition. While others see only today's remaining and transformed material structures, he sees the "ballet" movements within the area. This is due to his own experiences as a worker there.

Class is a social identity which is based on common experiences, practices and memories. And in focus group interviews with a number of workers, a class-related sense of place became especially obvious. This is because within a group of workers with similar experiences a common sense of place is developed within the narratives, as the memories of each worker provoke additional memories from the others. Within the interviews a common narrative of the group develops and memories of common experiences and practices in the former work place (which, with reference to Bourdieu, are considered here as class-related) are generated. Five male ex-MAN workers, all over sixty, consider the transformation of the factory site as a place where a sense of absence is evoked. In swapping memories of the past, they express a shared relationship to the plant area and its former condition. By remembering its exact former appearance and what is now lost, they express their common emotional relationship to the plant (Figure 5.6).

> Paul: Of course the site has changed substantially. After all much has been sold. (...)
>
> Oliver: To clarify what has changed – today, if you go out onto Vogelweiherstraße and straight on and then turn right, there is a short

length of wall close to Gugelstraße that has been knocked down. But back then, the wall was intact, all the way up to (...) Frankenstraße, and to Katzwangerstraße.
Paul: Up to the administrative building, right?
Oliver: And where there is no wall anymore, all that used to be part of the site. It all belonged to MAN – and now it's all gone. (...) The place where the administration for the entire MAN company in Nuremberg used to be – that's all been sold, everything is gone. Everything's gone. There, where the Frankencampus is, all that used to be the MAN administrative building.
Manfred: For the entire MAN company in Nuremberg.
Christian: And the old administrative building – the front building, doesn't exist anymore. There's only the Klett left. The entire brick building is gone.

By sharing their common memories within their conversation, together they awake the haunts of walls and buildings. The now absent former structure is born again through the common memory of the former workers. And these memories also trigger recollections of social relationships within the

Figure 5.6 The statue of Mr. Cramer Klett, now in front of the newly erected Frankencampus (photo taken by Lars Meier).

workplace, former working routines and everyday body movements, all of which are expressed in the interviews.

By also conceptualising class as a specific kind of experience that is expressed in personal histories, it is clear that the former workers are aware of their class identity, when confronted with their former work place, and when they consider what is now absent. Karl's strong emotional relationship to the Maxhütte and his feeling that this was his company articulate Karl's sense that he was not just a number or a working body. That this view of his role in the company was an illusion, or a false consciousness of his class situation (Marx and Engels 1970), became obvious for the former worker, during the encounter with the destroyed or heavily transformed factory, which happened without his approval.

For the former workers, their everyday experiences at the work place were not those of a number, or simply of a working body. They look back on their integration into a community where, as well as being a worker, each was an individual and not just an anonymous number. During encounters with the work place today, the haunting of such yesterday's everyday experiences appears – involuntary and painful. They are nostalgic hauntings of a former better and harmonious time, which effectively hides the logic of a capitalist production mode. But this is in sharp contrast to the manager's decision to close the plant and dismiss the workers, at which point it became obvious to them that they were also simply numbers in a capitalist economic logic.

Some argue that work has lost its relevance to identity in late capitalism. Ulrich Beck has used this argument to see class as a "zombie category" which though still alive in theory (Beck 2000), is dead within the reality of individuals in flexible and insecure labour markets. But Karl remembers common experiences of work – demonstrated also by his inclusion into the place ballet and still vivid in his memory – which demonstrate the opposite. Namely that work is essential for the development of class identity via shared labour experiences. Against the thesis that work has lost relevance for identity, the continuing relevance of class to income or health, and to everyday experiences as well as the concept of the self, is demonstrated in diverse studies, as in this chapter. MacKenzie et al. have shown that it is particularly those workers who have especially demanding and dangerous jobs – steelworkers for instance – who develop an emotional attachment to their work (MacKenzie et al. 2005). This often goes hand in hand with a need to take risks as part of their masculine identity, and is a fundamental part of certain jobs for men (Williams 1993). In Karl's memories these common work experiences are located at a specific place, the Maxhütte, where work experiences were also place experiences – inclusion into the place ballet for instance, and an actual sense of place.

Conclusion

Avery Gordon writes that: "Haunting is a frightening experience. It always registers the harm inflicted or the loss sustained by a social violence done in the past or in the present" (Gordon 2008: XVI). It is such a loss sustained by a social violence that has befallen these workers, with the closure and tearing down of their workplaces. For them, this violence comes to life once again today, through the haunting of what was there before and the emergence of a painful contrast between the former and current state of their work places. Using the metaphor of haunting, the loss and the social violence experienced by the workers upon the closure of their companies, it becomes palpable. The term social violence is used because these people had no say in the transformation of their workplaces and were treated purely as functioning workers within the companies. They once believed, with grave misapprehension, that they were more than that, but again and again, the haunting spectres of today make it clear that this was not the case. This situation lays bare the former workers' belief that they were not just numbers in the production process.

It is a common practice of workers today, to encounter a haunting of former times, together with former colleagues; either at the former workplace, or by narrating individual but similar memories. The emotions expressed in the workers' narratives are a product of a specifically class-related sense of place. In the memories of female and male workers, class relates to a specific workplace, or, more precisely, to what was there before the place was transformed. The haunting from former times, encountered by workers today as they remember their working lives and visit what is left of the former workplace, brings back memories of a better past. The workers' mourning for the loss of what was there before and is now absent is an emotional expression of class. Confronting the haunting today is therefore also a productive process. Engineering a direct confrontation with the transformed place today is a strategy devised by the workers, not only to cope with their loss, but also to ensure their own identities as members of a workers' class with an emotional experience.

The haunting has specific characteristics. It is painful, arrives involuntary and is repetitive, as it haunts again and again. But the haunting in this chapter is also seen as class-related as it does not haunt everyone. It affects only those with a specific, class-related experience and sense of place. This chapter has explored the role of social class in shaping a sense of place. Far from considering the workplace as solely economically driven, it shows that this is where a worker's class-based sense of place can be seen. The workers' own experiences at these places and their inclusion into a community have brought about the development of a sense of place. For the worker, the workplace became their friend, or "a second family." With the help of life story interviews, a sense of place normally hidden within the strictly economically determined narrations of working-class life becomes visible here.

In this chapter, places have been analysed as experiences and not as representations. But against the background of the chapter something on the subject of representations can be learnt: the workers sense of place, rarely considered in official representations of transformed workplaces, might be useful for improving social justice. On that note, the workers' memories of their work places, and the feelings and experiences that feed their sense of place, should be used to help document and demonstrate the consequences of transformations. This might also encourage social research to make more effort to view the work place as somewhere that is experienced in everyday life and to which workers have emotional connections, which are expressed within their sense of place. Everyday geographies, places and identities are not without a past, and it is through the haunting experienced by workers that this past and the social violence that may have happened can be seen and remembered.

Notes

1 Sulzbach-Rosenberg is a town shaped by mining and steel production that is 50 km away from Nuremberg.
2 The Maxhütte started its blast furnace in 1864. The location, in Rosenberg, was selected because of the nearby ore deposits and because of its position near the railway line between Nuremberg and Regensburg. Following the opening of the Maxhütte the number of inhabitants in Rosenberg rose sharply and in the following decades it dominated the nearby region. In the 1960s up to 9,000 people worked in the Maxhütte and around 95% of the workers were members of the industrial workers union. From 1981 the workers struggled against job losses and the threatened closure of the plant. Demonstrations and strikes were widely supported by inhabitants of Sulzbach-Rosenheim. Since, after its first bankruptcy, in 1987, the Maxhütte was temporarily partly owned by the federal state of Bavaria, its closure was also of political relevance. After the final closure of the Maxhütte in 2002, a separate pipe plant (Rohrwerk Neue Maxhütte) continued to function and is still open and working today, employing around 450 people. The development of a new industrial area in the 1980s also lowered the mono-industrial dominance of the Maxhütte in the region.
3 See also the "sidewalk ballet" by Jane Jacobs (Jacobs 1992).

6 Nostalgia and practices of resistance in public spaces

The general social relevance of the possibilities as well as the restrictions provided by the public space has been analysed in the course of history (Habermas 1991 [1962]; Sennett 1978). However, everyday experiences in the public space are also differentiated socially and are dependent on the social position of those being in the public space. The narrated memories of how the public space has changed attribute special relevance to the narrator's social position. Whether policemen on duty, young skateboarders, toddlers and their parents, homeless or bank managers – not only do they all have different requirements as to how the public space should be designed, they also be in the public space in different ways. This involves be in the public sphere also for such practices that were not intended when the space was planned or that even contradict design intentions. I investigate such practices of resistance (Scott 1985; de Certeau 1988) in the face of powerful strategies, which are expressed in discourses or in the structures materialised in the space, in the form of narrated memories of everyday practices of a social environment of manual workers. This chapter analyses the difference between the nostalgic memories of the workers own past resistance practices in the public space and present-day practices of resistance in the public sphere, which they consider as practices of the others. It is an abjection (Kristeva 1982) of the other that is also part of the self of the interviewees. Unlike their own past acts of resistance, the narrators consider these practices to be strange and threatening and limiting their own involvement in the public space.

Resistance and memories

By focussing on narrated memories of resistance practices in the public space, this chapter follows on from research investigating the possibilities to be in a transformed public space for social encounters (Liggett 2003; Watson 2006; Frers and Meier 2007) with regard to the restrictions of the public space in the course of privatisation or supervision (Davis 1990; Sorkin 1992; Smith 1996), also taking into account practices of resistance (Altay 2007). Building on research showing that social practices and social control in public places such as parks are related (Low 1996; Low, Taplin and Scheld 2005), the analyses focussed on resistance practices as physical activities in the public space such as skateboarding (Borden 2001; Chiu 2009) or urban cycling (Sharpe 2013).

I look at the matter from a slightly different analytical angle, investigating resistance in narrated memories of such practices in the public space. For this purpose, I build on Michel de Certeau's concept of resistance. According to de Certeau, the way in which people be in and perceive the public space is not just the result of architectural planning, political decisions, socioeconomic development or social norms. He shows that there are also forms of being in the public space, both intended and unintended, which as practices of resistance are inconsistent with the originally planned purpose and thus challenge norms and rules. Frequently, de Certeau's resistance concept is considered contrary to Foucault, but Foucault, too, demonstrated that power goes along with resistance (Buchanan 2000). For a better understanding of the concept, it is helpful to take a look at de Certeau's differentiation of strategies and tactics. Strategies belong to institutions and structures of power, whereas individuals act within a context ruled by these strategies. In this context, they use tactics that may be opportunistic to the strategies or that may take the form of a creative resistance against those strategies. "In short, a tactic is an art of the weak" (de Certeau 1988: 37). De Certeau elaborates:

> many everyday practices (talking, reading, moving about, shopping, cooking etc.) are tactical in character. And so are, more generally, many "ways of operating": victories of the "weak" over the "strong" (whether the strength be that of powerful people or the violence of things or of an imposed order, etc.), clever tricks, knowing how to get away with things, "hunter's cunning", maneuvers, polymorphic simulations, joyful discoveries, poetic as well as warlike.
>
> (de Certeau 1988: xix)

De Certeau's shifts in his conception of everyday practices of resistance the focus very much on agency. By doing so, he developed a critique on those theories of discourses (Foucault 1969) and habitus (Bourdieu 1984) that he considers as systematically undervaluing subjectivity as a simple reflect to broader structural forces. This leaves some critiques to speak of de Certeau's work as one that is casting a desocialised view (Theodossopoulos 2013) and "presents an account that is much better described as a theology than a theory – rooted as it is in a universalist and universalising notion of the human spirit" (Mitchell 2007: 91). Taking this critique on board, I argue here for considering the biographic narratives on practices of resistance as social practices of a specific social group, that of workers. In this chapter I investigate such everyday practices of resistance in the public space in the narrated memories.

As I have shown in Chapter 1 the workers' memories are not independent from a general discourse of an epoch. Transformations of the socioeconomic and spatial structures are thus also reflected in the personal life and in the narrated memories of practices of resistance and experiences in a dynamic public space (Massey 2005). Hence, this chapter takes practices of resistance seriously in terms of their temporality and duration. They are understood as practices and memories of workers that are related to their social position today.

Within the biographical narratives abjections of something that exists within the self and that attracts and repels at the same time can be seen. Julia Kristeva's trope of abjection (Kristeva 1982) helps to understand the sharp contrast between the interviewee's nostalgic narratives of their own past practices of resistance considered as positively on the one hand, and the negative view on present-day resistances considered as practices of the others. The concept of abjection refers to the process of identity constitution of individuals and also of social groups. The abject signifies an ambiguity: an attraction and a repulsion that disgusts the individual. The abject is positioned between the self and the other and "threatens the unity/identity of both society and the subject. It calls into question the boundaries upon which they are constructed" (Oliver 1993: 56). With the abjection the temporality of resistance comes into focus. Unlike their own resistance in the past, the interviewees consider these practices of the others to be strange and threatening (abject) in the public space today. The narrations of resistance today refer to the own childhood memories of the own past practices of resistance as the abject.

Nostalgic memories of practices of resistance in the public space

Jens, a 42-year-old metal worker who works in a small metal processing business in Nuremberg, tells of his childhood memories:

> To begin with, there were no computers and no mobiles. (...) Well, we were outdoors the whole day from morning until night. Even during school time. We just were troublemakers. We just caused a lot of mischief. But not the kind of mischief young people are up to today. There were still some rubble sites even in Nuremberg. Left over from the war. (...) They were the best adventure playgrounds. Our generation has no allergies. We used to eat dirt and make mischief.

As demonstrated before locations and places are bound to biographic memories as places where one grew up and lived one's childhood (Tuan 1977; Jones 2005) or lived through traumatic events. Jens, too, links his childhood memories to playing on "rubble sites" in South Nuremberg, a war-time leftover.

> (...) ruins serve as an uncanny space amidst a familiar realm. But precisely because they are regarded as forbidden or dangerous spaces, they can become space of adventure, places in which unspeakable and illicit acts occur, places of unhindered adventure. Ruins possess an allure for

> those who want to escape the increasing official surveillance in urban areas and the watchful gaze of neighbours and parents.
>
> (Edensor 2005a: 25)

Such spaces of adventure like ruins, demolished buildings, rivers or woods described by Tim Edensor that are outside the direct surveillance of parents or other authorities are a recurrent theme in the narrated memories of adolescence and childhood of the workers in South Nuremberg. They serve as spaces linked to tales of adventure in the memories and form a separate genre. Various studies have shown that children create their own spaces when playing and are thus not limited to the spaces determined and assigned by grown-ups (Jones 2000; Elsley 2004).

Such adventure plays like playing at railway underpasses are a central element in the narrated memories of the interview partners. One interview partner showed me such a place after our interview to give me an impression of the spaces that were important in his childhood (Figure 6.1). Another example of such adventure plays is to ride around one's bike unattended and boisterously. Sixty-year-old Andrea, a former warehouse clerk in a large electronics company, recounts:

> At age eight or nine, when you get your first bike, well we just rode around on our bikes. In the area near us down there (...) where there are

Figure 6.1 Railway underpass with graffiti one interview partner showed me as a place of adventure he roamed in his childhood (photo taken by Lars Meier).

> the sports grounds now, this was all still a little wooded back then. And later there as a child, quite ingenuous, you know.

Besides more extraordinary forms of resistance in the public space, Certeau focusses on activities which are not special but frequent everyday practices and which virtually go along with an everyday use of the public space. Practices such as cycling or partying on the pavement or in the streets, but particularly the more obvious and unconscious resistances such as the liberties taken when being out for a walk (random strolling, making a detour and straying off the path) (Lee and Ingold 2006; Moles 2008) challenge ordinary models of acting as well as the planning strategies and established structures based thereon. Memories of such bike rides into the woods out of the parents' sphere of influence can thus also be understood as tactics of resistance. Besides such trivial everyday tactics in which they experience their own room to manoeuvre, the workers also included special forms of resistance in their nostalgic memories. Jens narrates:

> We tore a cigarette vending machine out of the wall with our moped once. And back then it was nicer somehow. There were those machines that had a drawer. You still know those, too. And the very old ones, if you remember, there were two of them. If they were worn out a bit, you have the pressure point, right before the pressure point, the next just slid down. And then you could, bang, bang, empty the entire store. And then there were the others. You could push back the drawer a little. And then you could reach in there and pull it out. There were those two. And that was eliminated then. They put in those jagged metal plates so that you would tear open your fingers. Well, you know, but that was nice.

Paul Willis shows that it is subversive practices and minor rebellions in particular that not only reject school and the learning processes taking place there, but that also enable that "working class kids get working class jobs" (Willis 1977). According to Willis, the identity-related practices are crucial to produce the identity of a male working class, which is created not only in school, but also in the public space by means of tactics of resistance. Jens recalls with nostalgia the options he used and which he describes as being relevant to form his identity, that is also a male identity, in retrospect. He narrates the violation of allowed limits as his personal development history and in his narrative he considers to have proceeded in his development as a result of the institutional punishment of his practices of resistance. Jens narrates:

> You don't forget it when the police take you home. Or when you are grounded at home. Though we didn't really learn anything from it. All

> we learned was to act faster and run faster. (laughing) Yeah, but still. We got smarter at some point and then it was just over with it. (...) And once you start an apprenticeship, there are other things that matter.

But practices of resistance can also come at a high price which depends on the temporal, spatial and social context in which they occur. Jens' memories of his acts of resistance are also memories of another temporal context with a transformed "structure of feeling" that is the culture of a specific social formation with its specific conventions, values and perceptions (Williams 1977). Because in the present "the price of resistance, of standing by the dignities of an old order in which working class people had some worth, has become huge" (Charlesworth 2000: 153). This is why Jens' narrative concludes with a story of transformation. He describes his past practices of resistance as a necessary development that helped him learn how to deal with risks and conflicts, but also, as he puts it, to learn such rules and values that are important for him in his present social position as a journeyman locksmith who instructs and trains apprentices. Jens narrates:

> It was nicer somehow. It's as though you witnessed the remainder of a past time. Today, I'm afraid of the generation that is growing up. They only sit in front of their computers. We are still capable of dealing with it. Because we are used to talking with somebody face to face. And also to have a fight with the person. And also to brawl and kick the other person in the ass if necessary.

Violence is not described as a negative experience or as an expression of social anomie in this narrative. Quite to the contrary, Jens speaks positively of violence as a form of learning to deal with a social conflict. The narrative describes the previous physical conflict in the public space as a source of learning the social conflict that has a positive connotation; it is a skill that is lost today in Jens' view. Interviewee's memories of their childhood are characterised by a nostalgic view about former possibilities of resistance. In their narrations the interviewees express practices of resistance in public spaces positively as a childhood play. The former own practices of resistance are presented with a positive tone and as learned abilities and embodied tactics of resistance. This embodied knowledge is seen as being useful for today too.

Memories of using and creating other spaces are narrated as nostalgic adventure narratives of one's own childhood and that depict a harmonically idealised public space. Space is a central element of the sentimental feeling of having lost a better time which is expressed in the concept of nostalgia (Boym 2001). This is because home is a "spatial imaginary" linked to specific notions and memories of spaces (Blunt and Dowling 2006). The narrative of having lost a better time is phrased not only by Jens in the previous interview, but also by Heinz, a 70-year-old former locksmith who delivers the following childhood narrative:

> The good thing was my parents were never afraid for us children when we went out in the morning and came back in the evening. No, they knew them [others] were looking out, we were in the woods. There weren't any bad people back then, you know.

Heinz puts his memories of his former carefree life in the public space in contrast to the present-day situation. Heinz has memories of a rural community in the city, of an imagined harmonic community where the community assumed responsibility for the children in the woods, which does not exist for him anymore today. Idealised childhood places are frequently associated with living in a rural space, which is depicted as an antipole to the public space of the city. In "The Country and the City" (1973), Raymond Williams analysed this myth of a rural space of harmony and naturalness in English novels and showed that social conflicts, class conflicts and resistance against a ruling order are suppressed in favour of an all-embracing social harmony. He puts it as follows:

> an idea of the country is an idea of childhood: not only the local memories, or the ideally shared communal memory, but the feel of childhood: of delighted absorption in our world, from which, eventually, in the course of growing up, we are distanced and separated (...) this structure of feeling is powerfully expressed, and we have seen how often it is then converted into illusory ideas of the rural past: those successive and endlessly recessive "happy Englands of my boyhood."
>
> (Williams 1973: 138–139)

In the interviewees' narratives, nostalgia appears as the sentimentality for such an idealised socially harmonic home, which existed in South Nuremberg in their memories and which was associated with the use of the possibilities the public space can provide. They characterise the public space, in which their practices of resistance took place in the past, as a solidary and harmonic community. Jens remembers a community that was capable of resolving conflict based on specific norms and values to bring about a harmonic conclusion:

> We beat each other up, we were buddies. In the morning, you got your ass kicked by the boy next door. At midday, you kicked his ass. And in the evening, you got together for a beer.

The narrators' remembered practices of resistance in the public space were also processes of making place, the "way to broadcast and assert a collective identity" (Gill 2010: 1157) and thus to occupy the public space by showcasing one's own identity and rules. The narrated memories describe the others, the then migrants, as having adjusted to the dominant rules imposed by the German workers in South Nuremberg (see also Chapter 7). Jens tells of such an adjustment:

> It used to be better in the Südstadt back then. Well, you know, foreigners were never an issue. We already had them back then. But they behaved differently. They behaved totally differently. When I was still small, the Turkish father, who worked with Siemens then or something, you know. He could speak broken German, but his son, Bülent, he talked Nuremberg dialect fluently. They still tinkered with their cars. That was back then, they still tinkered with their cars and they were cool. And played football together and for the rest they were troublemakers like us.

The interview partners repeatedly contrast the memories of their activities in the public space and their use of the possibilities offered by the public space for playing, for strolling around aimlessly, cycling in the woods or adventurous roaming of rubble buildings with the situation today. Andrea puts it as follows:

> Today, I wouldn't dare allow a child go into the forest. But, er, back then it was safe for children to play there, you know.

When looking at the present-day situation, the interviewed workers emphasise the restrictions and dangers of the public space. This is in line with a generally growing anxiety of parents regarding their children's play in the public space which has a concrete impact on the way children play in and use the public space, and limits their mobility beyond their parents' sphere of influence (Valentine and McKendrick 1997; Foster et al. 2014).

Contrasting an idealised past with a difficult present situation is a key element of the nostalgia concept and of the workers' memories. The memories are of a public space as a place of encounter of a community of solidarity in which the individual could feel safe, as there were no "bad people" as Heinz remembers. Even though experiences of violence also appear in the narratives of the public space, and as Jens put it, you "kicked his ass," in hindsight this is not contextualised as menacing or as an expression of social anomie which restricted one's use of the public space. In the retrospective narrative, the practices of resistance of fighting physically in the public space in the past become practices of socialisation in a public space that was determined by the rules and values of one's own cultural practices.

Practices of resistance today – insecurity and diversity

The workers' memories of a public space that allowed them to perform their own practices of resistance correspond to the sentimentality for an idealised home to which they cannot return, because not only the public space has changed over time, but also their own social position.

> (...) nostalgic formulations of a lost public space themselves constructs an idealized perspective. (...) who were the public of these lost public spaces, who was included and who was excluded, and for whom were these public spaces formerly more public.
>
> (Bridge and Watson 2003: 374)

The feeling of having lost the possibilities to use the public space also puts into question the feeling of emotional closeness and belonging to the public space today. The workers consistently put the memories of their past resistance practices in the public space in contrast with the public space as it is for them today, which they frequently depict as threatening and restricting their present-day use of the public space.

The use of public space also varies over the course of people's lives (Elsley 2004). Narratives of older workers include memories of their own youth in public space. In their narratives, the workers no longer use the public space today for their own practices of resistance, but rather as a space that needs to be traversed quickly and out of necessity. The public space has been transformed from a space of staying to a space of moving.

Andrea tells me that "I am afraid until I get home" whenever I go to the movies these days. It is a feeling of insecurity in the public space as it is specific for a female experience of the public space. Her narrative expresses a transformation of her feeling safe in the public space. This change took place from a remembered feeling of security in the past to a feeling of insecurity today. She narrates:

> It is as I said much cultimulti going on over there in the Südstadt. Back then it still was a bit quieter. Now you can't even go down in the underground there in the Kaufhof area, because there is such horrible folk down there. And so aggressive, too, many have been mugged down there. Well, I don't see anything positive left in the Südstadt.

Andrea explains her feeling of anxiety with the increased diversity in South Nuremberg which she deprecatingly refers to as "cultimulti." As demonstrated in Chapter 2 the Nuremberg population have become more diverse in the last decades. This is especially true for the southern districts of Nuremberg. Since the 1960s the number of people migrated from other countries and the countries of origin have increased. The rise in social diversity goes along with changed and more diverse social encounters, for example, on the bus (Wilson 2011), in parks or in the street (Valentine 2008; Leitner 2012). Modern Western societies as in Nuremberg "exist as gatherings of strangers" (Amin 2012: 1). After work, the white industrial worker in South Nuremberg encounters the female student sitting in a modern café, well-trained service-sector employees and engineers having lunch at a kebab stand or Chinese restaurant. Young men stand in front of mobile phone shops while people in older age sit on park benches at Aufseßplatz, children play on playgrounds, veiled women pass by a church or social scientists eat pizza.

Figure 6.2 Encounters at the May festival at Aufseßplatz (photo taken by Lars Meier).

The former industrial workers' district with white German workers is no longer clearly recognisable as such today. Many have climbed up the social ladder and moved to the suburbs. People from different milieus, of different origin, gender or with different work experiences encounter each other in the street and at central squares such as Aufseßplatz (Figure 6.2) or Maffeiplatz. Elijah Anderson describes such public places as a cosmopolitan canopy. According to Anderson, they are places that encourage the individuals to show their cosmopolitan skills and so enable "for diverse strangers to encounter one another in a relaxed context" (Anderson 2011: XVII). The interview partners, in contrast, do not experience the encounters with strangers as relaxed but as associated with uneasiness, or in Andrea's case, with a feeling of anxiety of the stranger and his or her practices of resistance.

The feeling of anxiety is dynamic and is related to the specific temporal, spatial and social context. In their narratives, the interview partners project their anxiety especially on an "unpredictable stranger." It is a stranger "who is Other to one's Self, an individual who does not share one's own approach to life, one's principles and sensibilities" (Lupton 1999: 13). As Simmel has demonstrated strangeness is a form of interaction (Simmel 1971a [1908]). Due to their encounter with the stranger, the interviewees experience insecurity, because the stranger has an ambivalent status of orders and thus challenges securities, since: "the stranger is neither friend nor enemy (...) we do not know, and have no way of knowing, which is the case" (Bauman 1991: 145).

This liminal status of the stranger can generate feelings of insecurity or even anxiety.

The fear of the strange other is also an externalisation of undesired aspects of oneself – of the abject (Kristeva 1991) – as can be their own past resistances in the public space during adolescence and expressed in childhood memories. From a sociological point of view, the workers' nostalgic view of the public space and their own resistance in the public space in the past is related to their social position in the present. Because:

> Nostalgia, like the economy it runs with, is everywhere. But it is a cultural practice, not a given content; its forms, meanings and effects shift with the context – it depends on where the speaker stands in the landscape of the present.
>
> (Stewart 1988: 227)

This angle has changed. For instance, Jens speaks of how he sees the practices of resistance today, namely, as practices of the strangers.

> Those blithering multi-culti advocates, they should live in the Südstadt or in Gostenhof, for half a year only. Then they would stop drivelling. Those saying things like that, they usually live in Erlenstegen and have it quiet. They can say that easily. It doesn't happen on their doorstep after all. But there are things going on there. It's just a lot going on there. They haven't got a clue what's happening there. That the police don't show up at all in some places. What there, ecstasy or other stuff going on with Turks, there is a pub brawl, I watched from my window once. That's opposite of my place. They throw him out. Brawl, then 15 minutes of quiet. Then he returns high on "H" or what the hell, a crowbar in his hand and demolishes the outside mirrors and windscreens of each car in the Südstadt down Pillenreuter Straße.

As social complexity increases in the public space, the old order is put into question for Jens, Andrea and the other industrial workers. For example, noise and disorder, i.e. the expression of practices of resistances, are referred to as practices of the others and are associated with the increased social diversity in the narratives. Andrea further:

> I don't like this crazy noise in there. And I don't like this multi-culti stuff either. That's just too noisy and too much for me. It's not my thing.

Herbert, an 81-year-old former electrical engine fitter, also links the loss of order to the increased social diversity in South Nuremberg in his narrative:

> what bothers me maybe a little is the young people, see? The younger people, they don't have much sense of order. That is little discipline, see?

> The throw their milk cartons on the street. On the pavement and paper and stuff. That wasn't like that at all in the past. There are other things now (...) that bother me, that is, well, er, got to accept it. I do accept it after all. That is, you know, there are so many foreigners in the Südstadt now.

Mary Douglas shows that dirt and pollution are social orders, which illustrate that something is out of place (Douglas 1966). This forms a link to the construction of the stranger whom the interview partners also consider to be out of place, as disturbing the order. By describing the uneasiness experienced in the public space today, a nostalgic view is cast on a public space that is remembered as safe and harmonic in the past where resistance practices were their own practices and as such did not challenge the order. The strangers' practices of resistance are contrasted with this in the interviewees' narratives, polluting the order.

The hazards which the interviewees attribute to the public space today are associated in their view with the dissolving of a formerly harmonic community and the increased diversity in the public space. Their insecurity to frequent the public space is associated with a more general insecurity regarding their own social position. The strangers' resistance practices today contrast with their own past resistances and have the possibility to challenge and thereby pollute the old orders (Douglas 1966). In today's public space in the Südstadt district of Nuremberg, people who migrated are more visible in the public space and perform place making in the interviewees' narratives and are thus also present on footpaths and squares.

Parallel to the transformation of South Nuremberg into an urban area of diversity, the resistance practices in the public space have become cultural practices of the others that challenge one's values and norms. The contextualisation of the narrators' own practices of resistance as an expansion of spaces of use and as a positive socialisation experience contrasts with the contextualisation of the practices of resistance in the public space today. They are constructed as dangerous practices of strangers, making the public space today unsafe from this perspective and for the interviewees restrict the spaces of use and reduce the complexity of urban experiences in the public space.

Conclusion

Practices of resistance have a temporal dimension with regard to the process and the duration of their execution, to the context in which these practices are performed and in which they are remembered and narrated.

Narrated memories assign tactics of resistance – as conceptualised by Certeau – a different status. They are not innocent practices, but they also express a social positioning. Nostalgic memories of such practices and of the public space are always also an expression of such a social position, as "there is a multiplicity of meanings to nostalgia, many of which depend on who mobilizes the desire to renew a relationship to the past" (Angé and Berliner 2015: 7). The interviewees' childhood memories of practices of resistance can be considered as embodied tactics of resistance that evoke an experience of the abject when they come together with practices of the others that are negatively marked.

As South Nuremberg has transformed into a district with more diversity and with a loss of the status for those whose cultural practices defined norms, the workers' perspective of practices of resistance has changed, too. Narratives of conflicts or brawls in the public space today are characterised as menacing practices of resistance of the strangers. The narrated memories of own experiences in conflicts and brawls in the public space in the past, in contrast, are described as practices that construct an identity. Jens tells me:

> There used to be mass brawls sometimes. But if you were down, you weren't kicked anymore. That was the rule. And always the same number of people or you leave it alone. There was an ethical code. But you lived through this and you often had a black eye or whatever. But you knew who you were. You knew who you are and what you are capable of. Who you can take on and who not. You knew your standing in society. Finding one's personality I call it. And that is missed out today.

Not only is the public space dynamic (Massey 2005) but also the memories of the public space and the resistance practices taking place there have a dynamic and a temporal dimension, because: "memory is a process and not a thing" (Olick 2008: 159). The status of practices of resistance may thus change over time: own resistances narrated with nostalgia become menacing and dangerous practices of the strangers today. This contrasting gives the own resistances the character of social distinction (Bourdieu 1984) since they are valuable practices for the purpose of socialisation that contrast with the polluting practices of the other.

Part III

Community transformations and social encounters

7 Community transformations I

The nostalgic view of the former established

It is not easy to reach the apartment of Peter an 81-year-old trained toolmaker, who worked in the manufacturing company MAN for decades. After leaving the tram in South Nuremberg, I cross a bridge over a heavily used four-lane highway and reach the former residential cooperative Werderau. It takes me some time to get oriented in the narrow streets. I remember an urban planner who told me that Werderau is like an island in the city. Unlike in the more clearly arranged neighbouring quarters, in Werderau I walk along small winding roads with a mix of apartment houses and small detached houses with tiny front gardens. The architecture is different from the surrounding districts and the atmosphere is more quiet and calm with birds chirping in the background (Figure 7.1).

Figure 7.1 Small houses with gables and tiny gardens, Werderau (photo taken by Lars Meier).

But the social encounters on the streets are as varied as in the surrounding districts. I meet an older woman who walks slowly and helps me to find my way. I see children playing on the playground, white neighbours chatting over the fence of the front gardens and a man who migrated from Turkey sitting in an Italian snack bar while he tells me how nice it is in Werderau. But when I finally find Peter's three-room apartment in an apartment block, I learn that life in Werderau can be considered differently. He is sitting on a green plush sofa and remembers:

> Here it was wonderful because everyone knew everyone. They were all from the MAN. There was no stranger here. No other people because they didn't get an apartment. This was impossible. You knew the people, if you met someone on the street, then you had always something to talk about, about the MAN or about the apartments. There were not many problems.

In this interview sequence, Peter remembers how it was in Werderau for him. What he remembers is set into contrast to what he considers to be the present situation. For him, as in the narrations of other retired workers and inhabitants of the former housing estate of the nearby MAN company (manufacturer of engines, commercial vehicles and mechanical engineering equipment), social and "ethnic" diversity are considered mostly as a new phenomenon seen as disturbing the good old life in the Werderau when "everyone knew everyone" and when there "was no stranger" there.

Werderau was never as homogenous as these narratives suggest. But in former times every day cultural practices of different groups in Werderau were homogenised by the already established group through normative rules and regulations. What I will demonstrate in this chapter is that because of a transformation of an established-outsider figuration in Werderau, Peter and the other interviewees have lost their former power to define cultural practices as the norm what has cover up diversity.

This chapter thus demonstrates the dynamics of diversity in an urban setting, with diversity not being based on "ethnicity," gender or class but on more general differences in power. In this way, the chapter is a contribution to the discussion of the everyday diversity in urban settings, showing how the life story interview provides a powerful method for the construction, narration and experience of diversity and community, of difference and sameness, and how such narratives are mobilised as the long-settled response to the deepening of diversity.

Memories and an established-outsider figuration in Werderau

This chapter is mainly based on the analysis of two selected narrative life story interviews, those of Peter and Max, selected as representative of two types of interviewees (one who is still living in the Werderau and one who has decided to move) and of the main patterns of discourse identified in a wider body of interviews conducted in the area. Both men worked for decades as manual workers at the MAN before their retirement and have lived in Werderau. While Peter still lives in the area, Max decided to move away in 1999. In addition a focus group interview with five former MAN workers is considered here.

The workers' narrative life histories are about what happened in former times, very much from the perspective of today – how they make sense of their past and of the present. As explained before people use memories to interpret their lives and the world around them (Hacking 1995), and those memories are often linked to a place (Casey 1987). This is also true for heritage places, such as memorials, monuments or museums (Nora 1989; Frank 2016), and also for the everyday places and landscapes of individuals (Degnen 2005; Rogaly and Taylor 2009; see Chapter 5). Memories (see Chapter 1) are a social activity and a social product (Misztal 2003) and can also be considered as a binding force of a group identity (Halbwachs 1992 [1941]; Assmann 2005). It is through such memories that the territorial claims of a group are legitimised.

The workers contrast their nostalgic memories of former good times with today's situation in a transformed figuration. The theory of figuration, developed by Norbert Elias, refers to the interdependence of everyday activities of different humans as a system of power. A figuration is a social framework of individuals linked by rules, norms, values and positions. Here it refers to a system of two interdependent but opposing social groups. It is a dynamic system and its dynamic is due to contestations (Elias 1984) and organised around the discursive construction of self and other, as it is central for "race" and "ethnicity" (Hall 1999). Following this framework, "established" and "outsiders" are defined here by their status and by the power differences between those two social groups (Elias and Scotson 1965).[1] The concept of figuration is useful for this chapter because it helps to analyse the workers' narratives of community life in Werderau in a larger social setting. The nostalgia of personal memories demonstrates the transformation of the workers' social position within a specific figuration, that of established and outsiders in Werderau, which, as I will show here, shapes their narratives about diversity.

With Germany's growing labour demand in the 1960s, Southern European workers were recruited (first from Italy, Spain and Greece and later also from Turkey) mainly to work as low-skilled manual workers in the industrial sector.

They have been classified as "Gastarbeiter" (guest workers), despite the permanence of their immigration status. Instead of supporting integration, the aim of West German policy has been repatriation. In public discourse since the 2000s, Germany has more often been described as an "Einwanderungsland" (immigration country) with a focus on encouraging immigration of the desired highly skilled people from other countries. Nevertheless a "multiculturalism backlash" (Vertovec and Wessendorf 2010) has also found its way into public discourse. Nowadays more than one-third of the population in Germany agree with xenophobic statements (Decker et al. 2016: 34).

People who have migrated from Turkey tend to live in the traditionally industrial districts in the south and west of the city and are strongly represented among Nuremberg's less well-off populations. But in the last couple of years, classically middle-class outlying districts have seen an increase in the population with a migrant background. This is an expression of the social climbing of some, most of whom have lived in Nuremberg for quite some time (Stadt Nürnberg 2011a).

Werderau is a former working-class neighbourhood that has also seen an increase in the diversity of its residents. But social diversity is not a wholly new phenomenon. Already in 1979, 19 years before Werderau was sold to a private real estate company, 16.1% of the 4,590 inhabitants of Werderau were classified as foreigners (Stadt Nürnberg 1980: 110). After the sale, diversity had risen to 27.5% of the then 4,653 inhabitants (14.2% from Turkey) in 2010 (Stadt Nürnberg 2011b: 19) and to 30% in 2017 (Stadt Nürnberg 2018a).

This chapter demonstrates that the main impact of this change is not an increase of diversity, but a change in the powerful relationships between different social groups. Elias and Scotson have shown how an established-outsider figuration is created: their study of "Winston Parva" showed that newcomers from various regions of England did not, unlike the established residents, share the common memories which create internal cohesion, and demonstrated that it is the power imbalances between the groups which are responsible for dividing the two social groups, not supposed "ethnic" differences. My chapter shows how such a figuration can change. It demonstrates that the transformation of an established-outsider figuration comes with a breakdown of former regulations and rules that were previously asserted by the residential cooperative and that limiting the range of cultural practices has reduced diversity in the Werderau (Figure 7.2).

Furthermore, the chapter fills a gap in research on gentrification, seen as a general upward movement in neighbourhood social status. This type of research is usually analysed as a displacement of working-class people by wealthier people (Lees, Slater and Wyly 2010). In contrast, this chapter highlights the issue of migrant social mobility and its associated form of gentrification.

The loss of a golden age

Construction on Werderau began in 1911, following the "garden city" concept.[2] The aim of its founder, a director of the MAN company, was to make his workforce into a community. He wanted to create a sense of togetherness for the former farmers, by using an integrative spatial setting similar to their former villages. This is why some of the earliest buildings are like small farmhouses, and include garden plots for small-scale agriculture. This approach is reflected in the name Werderau. A Werder is the name for an island in a river, and also a marsh, dried up for settlement. Werderau is separated from the rest of the city by a main street and a railway line and also by its unique architecture. The area is characterised by a mix of small houses with gables built before the First World War, simpler neo-realistic buildings

Figure 7.2 Old sign saying that it is not allowed to play football, Werderau (photo taken by Lars Meier).

and larger apartment blocks built in the 1960s (Figure 7.3). In general, the arrangement of Werderau is spacious with small parks, quaint little streets, trees and gardens. The equipment of the apartments with bathroom and toilet was above average.

As demonstrated, the interview sequences on the Werderau are characterised by narratives on the loss of a socially homogenous community, with a strong internal solidarity. The differences between today and the past are shown by Peter and other interviewees as representations of the loss of a better era that is a part of a general myth of a former golden era of society (Williams 1973). This nostalgia, the idealisation of the past, is rooted in dissatisfaction with a chaotic present, and represents the desire for an imagined stable past that is celebrated (Watson 2006: 49) in the workers' narratives.

Figure 7.3 Apartment block, Werderau (photo taken by Lars Meier).

Nostalgia can mask past social divisions, and lead to a negative sense of the present. It is related to places where – according to the memories of the workers – idealised past experiences were made. The fixing of an identity to a place in the workers' memories is a matter "of power and contestation rather than of actually existing authenticity" (Massey 2005: 123). Nostalgia may also be the feeling of a loss of power. And it is this aspect of a loss of power in an established-outsider figuration that is a central issue in the workers' narratives in the Werderau.

In particular the recollection of former "good times" is connected to the daily experiences of a solidly close community. Peter remembers this community spirit in the neighbourhood. He argues that in the past, people shared a common experience of both work and Werderau. For Max, a 67-year-old former locksmith "MAN was a family." This family feeling and the sense of being a part of a work-related community is expressed by pictures of the MAN company, or by tin plates marking a work anniversary displayed in the living rooms of former workers.

Since the beginning of the 20th century working in a large industrial company in Nuremberg meant living close to other workers, in one of the company-owned housing cooperatives. Work in the MAN plant and life in Werderau was closely linked.

Because only those who have worked for MAN – as a worker or as a higher salaried employee – could live there. For the interviewees, this close link between work and residential quarters goes hand in hand with a spatial separation of these spheres from an outer world, by the walls of the company and the borders of Werderau. In their narratives, this was a close community who prided themselves on solidarity. Peter explained:

> In the building everything was absolutely clean. Everybody did their best to do their part, to keep everything in order. And at work, it was the same.

It is not only the former rural character of Werderau which led them to say that "we were a village" and express a strong local identification as "a Werderauer." Max remembers Werderau as where everyday life stayed within its borders:

> In the past, the rural character of Werderau was nice. You noticed more of what was happening around you. And who needed a newspaper, for God's sake? You went to the hairdresser and that's where you heard the news. That's how it was.

Georg Simmel (1971b [1903]) differentiates between village and urban life, using the multitude of impressions that a diverse urban setting has on its inhabitants. For Lofland (1973), the city is a "world of strangers"; encountering strangers is part of urban life. Taking this into consideration, it seems that interviewees remember life in Werderau as village life, rather than urban life, as demonstrated by the quote, "There were no strangers here." The four thousand plus inhabitants of Werderau at that time were not all personally acquainted with all the other inhabitants, but in their memories, the former social homogeneity is in sharp contrast to the current situation. To them, village life in Werderau was separated from urban life by its borders. While some sociological accounts have similarly considered worker communities of the 1950s–1970s as separated "urban villages" (Gans 1962), featuring a tight social community, socially homogenous and solidly united (Young and Willmott 1957; Taylor 1973), the homogeneity of working-class communities is overestimated in such a "composite picture" (Crow and Allen 1994: 26), neglecting external and internal differences and becoming a nostalgic construction of place (Blokland 2001). It is this nostalgic image of a better past which makes for a painful attachment to living and work places transformed by industrial decline (see Chapter 5).

Community homogenisation via regulations and control

Practices, rules and regulations also cover up internal differences, and generate a community which is built using the rules of the established residents who have the power to make those rules (like house regulations) and apply them to everyday activities. As people with different cultures adapt their practices to these regulations, the result is a homogenisation of the community.

Max remembers Werderau as a socially homogenous and harmonious community, as "a quarter purely for workers." From his perspective it seems that, because of its past social homogeneity, harmony and solidarity was everywhere in Werderau, complemented by the fact that "everybody knew everybody." The term solidarity is used by the workers in a specific manner. They are not referring to the support of a less powerful group by a more powerful group. To them, solidarity means solidarity within the group of established residents in Werderau – not solidarity of the established residents with the outsiders. This solidarity among the established inhabitants is a common protection of their own position in the established-outsider configuration, and an assertion their own cultural practices as a cultural yardstick to which outsiders must conform. Culture may be seen as a "struggle for meaning," in which the established inhabitants attempt to naturalise their cultural practices and establish them as the standard (Fiske 1987).

The interviewees describe Werderau as a small village, under the control of the MAN cooperative housing estate. This estate took care of Werderau, selecting its tenants, organising everyday life with strict rules, settling disputes between tenants, and taking care of the buildings and cultivating green public places. Peter remembers:

> If there were problems with the tenancy or something else, we talked to a representative from the workers council, and said there are such and such complaints. You cannot do that. Or please try to change that. And it [the solidarity] was the same at home as it was at work. Those who worked together and who knew each other, met and talked, and told stories from their work or whatever. It was just like a family.

He continues:

> There weren't many arguments. Unless somebody did not adhere at all to the house rules and then it was usually only a drunken man who wasn't able to do anything right. But that got sorted out and then it was quiet again. There was an office from the residential cooperation and there were also workers, a workshop, who did jobs, when repair works had to be done.

The established residents remember the former situation in Werderau in a very positive way, and also in the MAN company, where outsiders had to submit to their rules, thus confirming their power. These positive memories of tranquillity and harmony reflect the prevailing figuration at the time. Memories of the tranquillity of former times reflect the uncontested social position of the established residents back then. Changes in this context represent changes in the then established-outsiders figuration, threatening their own dominant position in Werderau.

The control exerted by the housing estate was accompanied by control from other inhabitants. This is expressed in the following sequence by Max, which is a reminder of the panopticon, as discussed by Michel Foucault (1991 [1975]), as a control of activities because the observed are aware that their activities may be seen.

> Werderau was a village of thousand eyes. You were seen when you came and when you went, and people saw whether you came home drunk or not.

In memories of former life in Werderau, the control of everyday life seemed to produce the kind of social harmony and homogeneity that could not be disturbed. However, these memories of the past are seen very much from the perspective of today.

The residential area of Werderau was never really as homogenous as it seems in the memories of the interviewees, and it was not completely separated from the outside world. The residents always had different regional origins, and held different jobs in the MAN (blue and white collar) or in Werderau. Class diversity was always important in the everyday life of Werderau. The blue-collar workers, the foremen, the white-collar worker and also some poorer people all lived in Werderau. Stacey argues against the idea of an internal coherent and fully integrated community at a local level and argues that it is more appropriate to analyse relations between different social institutions and assess their connection to wider society (Stacey 1969). But in the workers' memories, locality and community seem to be identical in Werderau. Even if a former social homogeneity of an imagined community is a myth (Anderson 1983), because community members could not know everyone at a personal level, even in a small village like Werderau, the workers comprise a community, with common memories and narratives. But it was also essential for concealing internal differences and divisions of community that everyday activities in Werderau were tightly controlled and regulated by the strict rules put in place by the MAN's residential cooperative. And this control was not limited to Werderau, but was also enforced in the MAN workplace. Different cultural practices were therefore ruled out, as shown in the following memories by Peter:

> If there were problems with tenants, or anything else, people were invited to the company workers' council, who warned them that they'd received complaints and explained that they must do things differently. (…) If there was a noise problem, the same thing would happen. In those days too there were strangers wanting to rent, and the committee of the residential co-operative would check the apartments they had lived in previously. Because sometimes it had been a disaster and the committee would say you cannot give them an apartment in our cooperative because they cause too much trouble. But if they had a good record, then

> they got an apartment. In those days, they all behaved decently because they were afraid to be kicked out.

Peter continues:

> Then the first Turks moved in. But we [from the co-operation] made sure that there were only one or two strangers in each house. This was to keep the feeling of togetherness intact.

Diversity was always an issue for the people in Werderau. This is clear in some interviews – although indirectly – and contradicts the picture painted by the interviewees, of a homogenous community in harmony. But in workers' narratives of former times there are not nearly as many strangers as today, and they are in most cases virtually invisible within these memories because "they all behaved decently because they were afraid to be kicked out." The outsiders are shown as ones who did not disturb the social harmony of Werderau village life, since they had to adapt their cultural practices to fit in with the rules of the established residents. Max remembers:

> Then [in the 1950s] the first strangers came. They were the Italians. At the beginning it was nice. Every week a farmer arrived, with a giant square cart filled with fruit and vegetables. He rang a bell and then he sold the produce. That's how it was in former times.

This is a perspective where a former village life of harmony and homogeneity was undisturbed by strangers, because they had to "integrate themselves," following the rules of the German workers, of the workers residential cooperation and of MAN. This sentiment is expressed in the following sequence from Ernst, an 80-year-old former MAN manual worker, who participated in a focus group:

> The Werderau is a multicultural quarter. Since the 1950s many strangers have been employed here and as long as it was under the leadership of MAN, they integrated themselves. But integration is the wrong word, they were inconspicuous because they had to work with German colleagues every day.

In former times the social position of the stranger in Werderau was that of an outsider, while the German workers were the established group, they defined how life was, in both working and public spheres of Werderau. They remember the outsiders and the former practice of constructing a figuration between outsiders and established as more or less invisible. But as this figuration between established and outsiders changed, the outsiders became more visible. Community is described in narratives which gloss over internal differences, and in the context of concrete rules and regulations, which prevented outsiders exhibiting obvious differences. But for the established residents, it's now clear that their former power in the established and outsider figuration was only temporary.

Diversity and a new figuration of established and outsiders

In 1998, following the sudden decision of the MAN company to sell the co-operative to a private real estate company (Telos), life in Werderau changed. After that more than half the 1260 accommodation units were sold to private investors. To compensate them for the sale of Werderau, the established tenants were given the right to rent their apartments for the duration of their lives, even if Werderau is resold. The neighbourhood and its image have changed since then (more white-collar workers, more single households and more people with a migrant background). What was once considered solidarity within shared life and work circumstances is now, from the perspective of the workers in older age, diminished. Peter said:

> The feeling of solidarity and the conversation during the day or evening is now lost.

The former MAN worker contrasts his memories of social solidarity with the situation today. And when looking back at the former housing situation, the change in social relationships becomes apparent. This change is primarily described as negative, as the loss of a community spirit and a weakening of social networks among the former established residents. Peter says:

> Now, everybody is alone. And nobody interferes with the affairs of others, because nobody knows each other and each others' circumstances anymore. (...) They have become loners. There is no solidarity. It has all been lost.

It was a community that was dominated by the powerful position of the established residents and supported by the rules and regulations of the MAN and of the residential cooperative. What was considered as solidarity by the former established, was actually a powerful solidarity within their own group, which was able to assert its cultural practices as the standard. But without the support of MAN and the residential cooperative, and with the upward social mobility of the former outsiders, the powerful positions of the former established are diminishing. As solidarity for the workers was as important to them, as asserting their cultural practices as standard, it is understandable that they consider the loss of solidarity to be a loss of power.

Unlike a young man with a migrant background who told me that Werderau was nice and that he liked living there very much (he has bought a small apartment) – because of the good social relationships with the neighbours, the building and garden structure and its proximity to his work place at

Figure 7.4 Pizzeria in front of larger apartment blocks built in the 1960s, Nuremberg, Germany (photo taken by Lars Meier).

MAN – the older interviewees take a different perspective. They talk about the loss of the good old days, where the community was tight and problems were solved smoothly, because of the power of the established as the leading group. With the loss of support for their own powerful position, from MAN and the residential cooperative, former established inhabitants moved away, and their social networks lost strength. The interviewees see this as a loss of solidarity. Peter told me about the changes in the former worker community, after it was sold by MAN:

> It is like a Turkish village now. The Turkish are now the second biggest group of people here, after the Germans. And they have different habits, which everybody is afraid of. (...) Those who were able to, have taken an apartment somewhere else.

In this excerpt, the interviewee complains about the changes in the place where he lives. It seems that he longs for a time when Werderau seemed to be a more socially homogenous area of MAN workers.

When the company housing estate was sold, the internal regulation mechanisms of the community changed: the former big regulators of social life, MAN and its housing cooperative office disappeared. This goes hand in hand with the disappearance of former and informal house rules (e.g. about the use of common areas and green spaces and about times when hanging washing out is acceptable) and the appearance of new inhabitants. It is connected to a feeling of loss of community and an inability to feel in touch with the new residents and the changed community.

But it's not true to say that there is now no community life in the residential areas; there are common playgrounds, benches and barbecue places where people meet. In Werderau today one can see groups of people eating and chatting in an Italian snack bar (Figure 7.4). On the other hand, however, the old bakery – a former meeting point – is closed. The interviewees see what they perceive as the loss of the community experience in Werderau or at their workplace in the MAN, as the main reason for the loss of a so-called solidarity. They also blame this for the fact that they no longer have the power to establish their own cultural practices as the standard to which others must adapt. For the interviewees, the social change is reflected in particular in the presence of newcomers who are considered and described as "strangers" because of their different work and life experiences. Peter says that fewer workers live in Werderau today:

> There are now less blue-collar workers who live here. But I guess now there are more white-collar workers and persons setting up their own businesses. For example, Italians selling ice cream and pizza. They are almost businessmen (chuckles). Yes, it has changed. And there are only a few people who work at MAN. Because they sold apartments to anyone who wanted one. It didn't matter who – as long as they had money. Done, finished.

And so, there was a change in the social structure of the residents in the Werderau, and social networks were weakened by people moving out. Some of the apartments were sold to people with a migrant background from Turkey and the proportion of non-MAN employees and of inhabitants with a migrant background rose.

After the sale, the workers felt betrayed by "the good father MAN." Now things in Werderau have become more complicated, as there is no longer a central organisation which takes care of it. The former powerful institution which controlled and regulated cultural practices has gone, and other practices are more visible. The residential area that was seen as relatively homogenous as a consequence of the control by the MAN residential cooperation has become more open and heterogeneous, with more interaction across the local borders of Werderau. Hermann, another interviewee in the focus group of former MAN workers, remembers:

> It's changed because now everyone can live there. Even people who never had anything to do with MAN.

As the former unifying force of being a MAN worker weakened, trouble between long-established and new residents increased (Berndt and Boeckler

2007). This development peaked in 2008, with a racist anti-foreigner initiative gaining 9.7% of the Werderau district votes in the local elections (in 2018 the AfD reached 15.7% of the votes in state election).

Older workers remember their former residence as a small place of peace and social solidarity. This is particularly because of the social homogeneity they experienced there, which they believed to be founded in their work experiences. It was a place where others had to adapt their cultural practices to fit in with the cultural standard of the established inhabitants and the institutions supporting them. These older workers find today's socially more heterogeneous residence as a place of demanding encounters and irritations. In their memories, the conflicts and disadvantages of a close social community as well as the social control of the neighbourhood are pushed into the background. And the opportunities offered by a heterogeneous urban community (Simmel 1971b [1903]) are seldom seen as such. Very long-term inhabitants of Werderau are especially likely to see the changes as negative. And they are upset by the fact that cooperatives are now open to people who are not working in the MAN plant, which in their view disturbs the social homogeneity of former times. Peter said:

> Living together is not how it was. You can see this if you go out of the apartment door. There are 20 pairs of shoes in front of the opposite door. This bothers us but if you ask if they could adapt a bit and put their shoes into the apartment like we do, they refuse. They say Germany doesn't belong to you.

Werderau is now an area where workers living there encounter many more people who come from elsewhere into this former workers' community. But it is not only the degree of diversity that has changed; the formerly invisible outsiders are now established, and able to buy apartments in Werderau. They are no longer outsiders who are subordinate to, and have to fit in with the standards imposed by the dominant established. Max explained how it is for him today to encounter his former apartment:

> On my way home I always drive through Werderau, where I used to live. I take a detour and take a look at what has changed. A Turk lives in my apartment now and today, if I look up at it, I can see that he has added many arches, with pompoms. I feel as though I never lived there. It just isn't my Werderau anymore.

In this sequence it becomes obvious that today in Werderau, established people who have migrated to Nuremberg have the power to "make place" (Gill 2010) and, by expressing and asserting their own cultural identity, to visibly change its former structure. Castles and Davidson have noted that this can "shock the majority group and confirm their view that the aliens are taking over" (2000: 131). In the case of Werderau, this is not a subordinate group practising a cultural expression. It is an expression of the power gained by the recently migrated, a new opportunity to act, resulting from a decline in the power of the formerly established residents. Place-making in Werderau is an expression of the transformation in the established-outsider figuration of the inhabitants. This is also articulated by Max:

> Many strangers ask that we integrate with them, because they do not want to integrate in Werderau. Those who arrived first were okay, because they were grateful. But the descendants, the second generation, they are different. You can see that just by looking at them – and their Mercedes' with AMG equipment and BMWs and so on.

Today it is the former outsiders who can afford to buy an apartment or a fancy car, while the Werderau older residents are often still renting their apartments. This can lead to feelings of losing their long-established social position. And this is something that is particularly triggered by the rising power of former outsiders, which can be seen in their ability to buy the apartments of the formerly established residents – and set their own rules.

Conclusion

By demonstrating how life story interviews contribute to the analysis of diversity in an urban setting, this chapter is a contribution to qualitative research on new forms of urban diversity.

Although others have discussed the opening up of Werderau and an increase in transnational contacts (Berndt and Boeckler 2007), this chapter focusses on a transformed figuration within a small urban quarter. This transformed figuration resonates with other descriptions of responses to diversity elsewhere. Paul Gilroy has argued that in Britain a "postcolonial melancholia" deriving from the "inability to mourn its loss of empire" gave a sense of coherence to British culture (Gilroy 2005: 102). My chapter takes a different approach from those studies representing members of white working-class communities in Britain as having racist resentments (as criticised by Ware 2008; Back 2009). In the case of Werderau, communities are created also by homogenisation processes implemented using rules and regulations that support the powerful position of the established. The breakdown of this force, as happened in Werderau with the sale of the company housing estate, means that the figuration between outsiders and established residents is subject to change. In their new role as those who are no longer the established, the workers' feelings of nostalgia are also yearnings for their formerly powerful position in Werderau. When MAN decided to sell Werderau, the established workers were helpless in the face of that decision. The former "good father MAN" no longer took care of them and no longer protected and supported their role as the established. The established residents came to realise that their former power had only ever been temporary.

The workers' memories of the transformation in the figuration between established and outsiders have had an impact upon their current considerations of their own social position within a figuration. As previously discussed, communities are not only constructed in narratives and in the imagination, and as shown in this chapter, we must consider practical rules and regulations as a homogenising force and a constructor of community. My chapter supports a critical view of the concept of "ethnicity," because "ethnicity" is a perspective on the world, rather than something in the world (Brubaker 2006). But as is demonstrated in this chapter, "ethnicity" is mobilised as a maker of difference and change between established and outsiders.

This chapter has also demonstrated the importance of a focus on social networks in a figuration (Wimmer 2004). I have shown that the power of the established was constituted by a strong social network which developed over generations. But the power of this network was reinforced by the rules and regulations of MAN and its residential cooperative, which supported and asserted the cultural practices of the established as the quasi natural standard to which the outsiders had to adapt. In retrospect, the established inhabitants interpreted their power and control over the cultural practices of the outsiders as a life of social harmony and solidarity. The sale of Werderau resulted in the loss of this organisational support, and also of the assertion that cultural practices of German workers should set the standard. The power loss of the established was also connected to the advancement of some of the former outsiders, and their stronger social networking (illustrated in the next chapter). The established now no longer determine which cultural practices are the standard and admissible as such. In contrasting their memories of former times with today, this loss of power becomes frustratingly evident for the German workers.

But their nostalgic perspective is different from that of former outsiders who look back on their social climbing without nostalgia.

Notes

1 The capability of the established-outsider concept is demonstrated also in recent research (Hogenstijn, Van Middelkoop and Terlouw 2008; Loyal 2011; O'Connor and Goodwin 2012).

2 The garden city concept was initiated by Ebenezer Howard in 1898. Beginning with the first garden city Letchworth in North London, garden cities were erected near other industrial regions worldwide, like in the USA (Crawford 1995), the UK (Hardy 2000), Australia (Freestone 1989) and Germany (Wolff 2012).

8 Community transformations II

The non-nostalgic view of a former outsider

At the end of a life narrative interview with 75-year-old Emilio in Nuremberg, he explained to me:

> I am now a nobody. A nobody because I am neither German nor Spanish nor… But, well, I have been here for 50 years, and I have lived in Nuremberg and worked as well. My language is not really German as I haven't learned it… I learned it by myself.

On first reflection, it is distressing to learn from an older man, looking back on his whole life, that he feels he is "now a nobody," but Emilio, a retired industrial worker, does not complain. He is aware of the possibilities of a mixed identity (Bhabha 1994), of being "neither German nor Spanish," and he does not express a desire for an idealised or lost home as is often considered to appear with migration. With migration, home is redefined (Al-Ali and Koser 2002) and a sense of belonging is related not to one place but to multiple sites (Ahmed 1999). Indeed, Avtar Brah (1996: 192) writes that:

> On the one hand, "home" is a mythic place of desire in the diasporic imagination. In this sense, it is a place of no return, even if it is possible to visit the geographical territory that is seen as the place of "origin". On the other hand, home is also the lived experience of locality.

Brah's concept of a "homing desire" points out that there is no possibility of returning to such an idealised home and indicates that not all people with a migrant background maintain an ideology of a return to a place of "origin." On the basis of an in-depth analysis of this case study – the life narrative of Emilio – this chapter explores this alternative, suggesting that people with a migrant background may sometimes avoid a nostalgic view of home and instead demonstrate a resilient and practical transnational strategy of home. Although it is often understood that ageing leads people to become more immobile (Wiles et al. 2009) and more focussed on locality, this chapter demonstrates the opposite tendency, namely, that, in older age and especially with retirement, people can also become more mobile than they were previously. This chapter thereby contributes to research on ageing examining the changing nature of community attachments in later life against the backdrop of globalisation processes (Phillipson 2007), in resonance with work on transnational mobilities in retirement migration (Gustafson 2001).

Emilio has lived as part of a transnational family since migrating to Nuremberg, by sending remittances or talking to his parents and relatives in Spain on the phone. But, with retirement, he was able to visit his children more frequently who were now living in different places in Spain. As his "homing desire" (Brah 1996) is not related to a locality but to his relatives – now living in different localities – it is demonstrated here that a "homing desire" can be also subject to change while ageing: Emilio has a stronger yearning for Spain today since his children left Nuremberg for Spain. Nonetheless, Emilio considers home to be located not only where his three children live in Spain, but also where his new family – a second wife and step-children – live in Nuremberg. Therefore, his "sense of home," after having retired as an industrial worker, is analysed in this chapter as an example of a member of a transnational family (Bryceson and Vuorela 2002; Parrenas 2005).

During his life Emilio has learnt to be "out of place" (Said 1999), "a nobody," and to adapt to transformed local social and spatial conditions in Spain and Germany. In consequence of these issues, this chapter demonstrates that today Emilio is non-nostalgic for a lost home: first, by illustrating the use of a life story method and of a single case study; second, by recapturing Emilio's life narrative as an empowering story of learning to adapt to transformations in his work and family life; third, by including the relevance of class to a sense of belonging, arguing that this may outplay the relevance of an emotional bond to a workplace; and, fourth, by exposing the importance of the inclusion into a transnational family for the concept of home among people with a migrant background in older age. Finally, in contrast to the nostalgic type in Chapter 7, Emilio's case demonstrates that upward social mobility can be accompanied by a new position in an established-outsider figuration.

An unusual case and the value of a single case study

The life narrative interview method is well established in migration research to analyse how people who have migrated make sense of displacement (Eastmond 2007) and how identities are reconfigured by migration (Kazmierska 2003). Life narratives have proven especially productive methodologically for those working with people having a migrant background of older age (Gardner 2002), because in older age the semantic memory (general knowledge about one's past including critical components of personal identity) can be better recalled (unlike episodic memory on specific personal events) (Kenyon, Bohlmeijer and Randall 2010: 214).

This chapter is mainly based on a single case study: the life narrative of Emilio. His narrative is an example of the relatively unusual non-nostalgic case and, as such, is contrasted with the more usual nostalgic type analysed in Chapter 7. It is selected as unusual precisely to examine the absence of nostalgia for an idealised home in the life narrative of a man in older age. Single case studies have a long tradition in the social sciences (Stake 2000) and are considered useful if the case is an extreme case, a typical case or a longitudinal case (Yin 2003). This method allows us to explore an in-depth illustration of social processes, but what makes the narrative of Emilio especially valuable as a single case study is that it is an unusual case that, therefore, allows us to challenge and expand the existing assumption (Flyvbjerg 2006: 228) that migration results in a nostalgic desire for an idealised home. In this sense, Emilio's narrative differs from narrations of German workers living in Nuremberg for generations or from those of people with a migrant background whose everyday activities are now focussed on Nuremberg and who are less involved in a transnational family today. Their nostalgia for a better past and a lost home is expressed by an emotional sense of place relating to a former workplace (see Chapter 5) or by a longing for a formerly social position as established within a transformed urban quarter (Chapter 7), both of which are markedly absent in the narrative of Emilio. He therefore allows us to explore an alternative to the dominant understandings of home in older age and, in doing so, also reveals those typicalities.

Being "out of place" and the absence of nostalgia for a lost home

For a number of reasons, Emilio experienced marginalisation from society in Spain during his youth. His memories prevent him from perceiving the "home" left behind as a place of desire, because Emilio remembers being excluded by specific political and social regulations in a particular time. He was born in Madrid and, after Franco's military putsch, his father, a leftist, was arrested. Even after his release, when Emilio was eight years old, he has memories of starving in Madrid and travelling frequently by train to his grandma who fed him. As a result, he remembers his youth as a steady struggle with the consequences of political regulation and learning practices of resilience against authority and poverty. The arrest of Emilio's father and the political situation in Spain forced him to learn to be independent and he remembers this with pride. In doing so, he learnt that he could not count on external structures to become skilled. Not being baptised, it was impossible for Emilio to go to a public school in Spain but he was forced to leave his private school due to financial problems. So, he started working as a saddler and, two years later, as a tinsmith for cars. In the meantime, he moved with his family from Madrid to a city in the Spanish-Portuguese border region and later to San Sebastian, where he married and his three children were born. His life story is a narration of not only frequent moves within Spain, but also of feeling himself incompatible with the powerful structures of political regulations.

Emilio's memories of his youth and childhood are in many aspects a narrated story of being "out of place" (Said 1999) and are not imbued with a longing for an idealised home or with ties to a specific place. This differs from childhood memories of the interviewees I identified as the "nostalgic type" (see Chapter 7), since their childhood memories are often nostalgic for an idealised past (Davis 1979) and located in an idealised home that no longer exists. Emilio's example shows that the potential development of home as "a desire" also relates to former social positions and experiences, and, since Emilio was forced to be on the margin of society, his life narrative now in his older age lacks any nostalgia for an idealised home in his childhood years. This is because a sense that the present is deficient in comparison to childhood memories – which is considered a condition for nostalgia (Chase and Shaw 1989) – is absent in Emilio's narrative today. On the other hand, more nostalgic interviewees told me about their personal advancement since the post-war years in Germany and regret the loss of manual industrial work in Nuremberg, as it presents a tougher challenge for them to adapt to new employment and socioeconomic circumstances. Unlike Emilio, they haven't had the experience of their sense of belonging being put into question so frequently. For Emilio the situation is different; agency in his life course is marked by his response to transformations.

Transformations and home – adaptations and senses of belonging

In the previous section, I argued that Emilio has learnt to adapt to transformations and to be "out of place" or "a nobody" during his life. His narration is, consequently, a story of success, rather than despair. It tells of his social advancement towards a well-paid occupation, the good qualifications his children received, and the development of his living in a transnational family with multiple localities of home. In this section, I will explore how Emilio's sense of home refers less to a concrete place and more to shared experiences of being an outsider and to the trust in his capabilities as a worker and provider for his family.

Between 1960 and 1973, around 600,000 people migrated from Spain to Germany. The then 26-year-old Emilio remembers his arrival in Nuremberg:

> That was 1961, the 21st of September, a Friday. Thursday we left and Friday we arrived, and then on Saturday we got the papers in an office of MAN [the engineering factory Maschinenfabrik Augsburg-Nürnberg]. I was occupied as a welder, even though this was not my occupation because that was tinsmith. Then as a welder.

Emilio explained that he was motivated to go to Germany because he wanted to earn money to support the education towards formal school graduation of his three children who had accompanied him, together with his former wife. He wanted his children "to become something better than I was." The decision to migrate to Germany was influenced by Emilio's desire for upward social mobility. This was a success as his three children received a formal school graduation, which still makes him very proud today. For many people with a migrant background the devaluation of their formal qualification due to regulations in Germany is experienced as a frustrating and discriminating challenge that questions their identity, but this is not a predominant issue in Emilio's narrative, which is instead focussed on his adaptation to the new situation. Of the day of his arrival in Nuremberg, he remembered that he had to follow and adapt to a strict regulatory process:

> We arrived in Germany by train after one and a half days of train journey and eventually we arrived in Cologne. There we all had to get off the train. We had to walk in threes to the dining hall to eat like in the military. Then we had to wait and they said were we would go. Then we arrived in Nuremberg, maybe eight or ten men. Then they came and took us all to the MAN. (…) We lived in residential rooms of the MAN. No shanties but nice residential rooms with warm water and showers. Then on Saturday we got papers in an office of the MAN and then on Monday we started.

After one and a half years he managed to change his job at MAN to the car repair shops, where he worked as a tinsmith, and then as welder and mechanic at the bicycle plant Herkules, that was later closed and demolished in 2004. Today, the area accommodates a car wash and some small companies, such as workshops or a bicycle store (Figure 8.1).

The nostalgic-type interviewees complain about the loss of their former workplaces and idealise former experiences at their workplaces. They even express a sense of home at their former workplaces by making regular visits, even though these places are heavily transformed or ruined. For them, the closing of a former plant considered by Gerda as "a second family" is "a shock" (see Chapter 5). In contrast, Emilio explained why he lacks such strong emotional bonds to his former workplace and does not consider it home-like:

> From my perspective, this is a kind of adaptation. (…) The transformation I don't worry about. It is gone. The company was anyway untradeable. (…) No thoughts. Once, before they closed the plant, I walked by with my wife and there were some people from Herkules, Germans that I knew from work in former times. They held a solemn vigil with a brazier. I talked to them. I felt nothing. (…) People complain about. But

Figure 8.1 Car wash on the area of the former Herkules plant (photo taken by Lars Meier).

> I always say it leaves me cold. Because if you watch TV like people get killed in a war like Vietnam. Or if I then see in Africa that hundreds … But because this is so close, the people don't care about the other. Maybe I have become hard, maybe macabre. I don't know, but it does not touch me emotionally.

Emilio switched between different workplaces during his long working life, so it comes as no surprise that he lacks emotional bonds to his former workplaces and does not consider them as a home. People have an emotional sense of belonging to the spatial settings of home, but the concept of a sense of belonging also relates to social identities. Belonging comprises two aspects that are often analysed separately: the feeling of being at home in a place (or multiple places) and the sense of a collective identity like that of class, gender, citizenship or "ethnicity." With this conception, I follow the insights of Antonsich (2010) who considers a "place-belongingness" as the personal feeling of being at home in a place and the "politics of belonging" as the discourse that constructs socio-spatial inclusions within a social group. Class is not only about the position in production, the access to resources or the share of capital, but it is also a cultural process through specific everyday activities and experiences that might also include activities within a transnational social field (Kelly 2012). Emilio does not narrate his class affiliation only by putting a focus on the social relations at a workplace, but his sense of belonging as a worker also means belonging to a social group of workers who are connected by a specific social position in the work process that spans different localities. Even though Emilio today says that he is a "nobody," his life narrative shows a sense of belonging to a social group that is defined by class and by a political consciousness of this position as working class. It is a social group that intersects with other groups defined by "ethnicity" or nationality. He said:

> For me it was natural to be leftist as a worker. (...) In the company, many foreigners worked there. I had good relations to all who were leftists. They came from many countries Greek, Turkish and others ... Italians. If there was a strike, then the Spanish, the Italians and the others stood in one block and the Germans stood inside. I said to them what is up with you we are outside and you sit inside.

In contrast to the German workers' narratives, Emilio has a different awareness of his class position. It is said that "intersections of class with ethnically-based identities in the workplace undermines [an overall] class solidarity" (Kelly 2012: 181), but that people like Emilio who have the status of "ethnic" outsiders develop a specific class-based solidarity within the group of "ethnic" outsiders. In Emilio's case, it is a process of a "class in itself" moving in the direction of a "class for itself" (Marx 1847). This is different from the German workers' class identity that is more hidden as it refers to a different tradition of class with reference to a specific national model of a welfare state, the Rhineland Capitalism of corporatist regulations with strong workers participation (Albert 1992). This caused an appeasement of class conflicts in Germany, which is different from other countries with different regulations and welfare state models like in Spain (Esping-Andersen 1990) and has an impact on the social identity dimension of class. For Emilio, the sense of belonging to the leftist working class, an example of a politics of belonging, is of relevance and criss-crosses a sense of belonging to a Spanish community. He explained that for political reasons the Spanish community in Nuremberg in the 1960s was divided between a group of Franquists around a cultural club, the "Centro Espanol" established with support from the Spanish embassy in 1961, and a group of leftists who organised themselves in a different club. Later both clubs merged. Emilio expresses his belonging to the working class and said about the relation to work after his retirement:

> If you don't work any more, you are a number that no longer exists. You cannot argue with the foreman or with the boss. You cannot claim more wages, you cannot do anything. It is a difference to work or not to work.

His retirement and the loss of his job put his sense of belonging to the workers into question for him. His feeling of being now a "nobody" not only has a national or ethnic implication. No longer being a part of the work process as a pensioner, he has also lost his sense of belonging as a member of working class that is settled between other classes and has to struggle together against the interests of the bosses.

Unlike the nostalgic type (Chapter 7), his sense of belonging to a class is not related to the former workplaces which he does not consider an idealised home. Emilio does not have a "place-belongingness" to his former workplaces, but his sense of belonging to the workers (the "politics of belonging," Antonsich 2010) is placeless. His home is not a workplace but – as demonstrated in the quote above – a sense of belonging to a transnational class of workers, more specifically to the workers group of leftist "ethnic" outsiders.

A transnational family: home, belonging and mobility in older age

It is said that older people spend more time at home and are less mobile (Smith 2009). Yet, by conceptualising home not as a single place but, rather, as a transnational social field spanning multiple locations, the opposite can be identified from the example of Emilio: after retirement, the mobility of a transnational family member may increase in older age and, certainly, Emilio is now far more mobile between Spain and Germany than he was before.

Emilio explained to me that originally he had wanted to go back to Spain after his retirement and for this purpose had bought a house but, as time went by, he sold the house and today he just travels there for longer visits. This change resulted when he created a new family in Germany, with his second wife and two step-children. Nonetheless, Emilio continues to visit Spain since his children have returned to Spain. His family-related sense of home has become more complex in older age. In Emilio's life, home is, therefore, not a single place, but different places with biographical significance that are complexly related through diverse attachments and connections. He currently crosses diverse local borders by travelling frequently to his three children in Tenerife, Barcelona and a small city in Catalonia, but also to a cousin and a niece of his first wife in San Sebastian. Besides regular phone calls, he frequently visits his family members in Spain for about three months every year.

Besides everyday material practices, such as communication, travel and remittances, Emilio's family relations are mainly interconnected by emotional relations (Salazar Parreñas 2008; Baldassar 2007), identity-related narrated memories (Chamberlain and Leydesdorff 2004). For Emilio today, as an older man, home is the localities where his family members live. As his children now live in Spain, his considerations have changed while ageing and he explained: "But now I have more and more yearnings to Spain" and to his children and grandchildren.

Transnationalism implies that migration does not mean to "substitute old homes for new ones in a straightforward transfer, but often to create an active social field between the two" (Ramji 2006: 646). His increased ability of being mobile since his retirement, allows Emilio to actually experience home (that is today a multi-sited attachment within a transnational family network) in different places: by being and physically experiencing a place and by staying in touch with the other places. It is his rise of mobility that today allows Emilio to feel at home, especially when he is not staying too long in one place but moves frequently within the transnational social field of his family.

Conclusion

For a long time, people with a migrant background in Germany have been considered likely to stay only during their working lives and to leave before or with retirement. This perspective was based on the assumption that the migrant's home is, and remains, their place of "origin." Yet, as argued by Brah (1996) and empirically demonstrated here through Emilio's life narrative, home also is the "lived experience of locality" and not only a "mystic place of desire" (Brah 1996: 192). Therefore, it is no surprise that many of the first so-called "Gastarbeiter" (guest workers) stayed longer than expected and aged in Germany because it became a home. There is still a lack of research on older people with a migrant background in Germany, but data demonstrates that the number has grown rapidly to 2.6 million (50–64 years) and 1.5 million (65+ years) (Hoffmann and Romeu Gordo 2016: 65).

The case study of Emilio contributes to the argument that diversity among older people in Europe has increased in general (Daatland and Biggs 2006; Kolb 2014). However, this chapter is also a call to analyse home with regard to different types and, specifically, to recognise a "non-nostalgic type" who does not idealise a lost home, as exemplified by Emilio. His life narrative illustrates the need to consider home and mobility of older people with a migrant background with respect to transformations during their lifetime, such as an active involvement in a transnational family (that might change over time) or former experiences of feeling "out of place" (Said 1999) at the place of origin. This chapter has argued that Emilio's experiences in a transnational family network, his lifelong sense of agency in learning to adapt to new locations and social conditions, due to several moves and workplace changes, provided him – as a man in older age – with a resource to handle further social transformations in Nuremberg (towards a service-sector city) more easily than those interviewees without such experiences and, thereby, he does not narrate a nostalgia for the loss of an idealised home.

Emilio's feeling of being "a nobody" now as a man in older age can then be understood not as a tragedy, but as a resilient statement of a mixed identity and of a home that spans different localities within his transnational family. Ahmed (1999: 341) identifies that migration leads to "a splitting of home as place of origin and home as the sensory world of everyday experience" and it was argued that with migration home also became a desire of an idealised past that cannot be realised (Massey 2005). However, as demonstrated with the example of Emilio in this chapter, home can also be a sense of belonging to a transnational social field of a family or a class. In addition, this chapter has demonstrated that home can transform while ageing. Emilio's former home of a member of a transnational class of "ethnic" outsider workers has partly been replaced by a home of a transnational family. Emilio is, therefore, an example of those cases with a migrant background in older age who challenges other findings that suggest with older age attachment to one place of home is strengthened and mobility is decreased (e.g. Rubinstein and Parmalee 1992).

Emilio's case shows that upward social mobility can be accompanied by a new and more powerful position in an established-outsider figuration – an explanation for his non-nostalgic view of a past in which he was an outsider.

9 Conclusion

I started this book with a quote from Walter Benjamin saying that our mode of perception is changing with transformations of society. During the lifetime of the interviewed workers, society and its socioeconomic and spatial conditions have changed significantly and this has impacted on the workers' narratives and how they express their perceptions of today. The workers' narratives have been understood in this book as today's narratives of the past used by the interviewees to interpret their lives in today's society. Their narratives are individual social positionings in social space today, expressing a class perspective.

The workers have experienced huge transformations in the economy and society as expressed in the local setting of Nuremberg. From the 1950s until the 1980s, older interviewees have experienced a huge growth in their purchasing power, in a welfare state with expanding benefits and strong workers' unions. Since then, they have experienced a structural change towards the service sector, automatisation and outsourcing; these changing practices coming to Nuremberg caused closure of some of the larger factories, loss of manufacturing and blue-collar jobs and a rise in the service-sector jobs. The generally increased marketisation in different sectors (health, pensions, housing, etc.), new regimes of work and management came together with general cuts in welfare support and changes in social policy. This has different local expressions in Nuremberg (e.g. privatisation of public and cooperative housing or a rise in the poverty rate) and in Nuremberg's local structure of feeling.

These transformations also found an expression in the representation of Nuremberg. The workers have experienced the change from a working-class city towards a representation of Nuremberg as a service-sector city – now attractive for professionals. The interviewed workers have to cope with a devaluation of their working knowledge, their physical labour skills and also with the consequences of a changed representation that brings them loss of status and of symbolic capital.

The interviewees cope with such structural changes, with the devaluation of their knowledge and loss of symbolic capital, through their nostalgic narratives. These narratives express a dissatisfaction with today and more specifically with their social position in today's hierarchical social space. However, the workers' nostalgic narratives are not only expressions of passive desperation or of negative responses to transformations but they are also currently active cultural practices.

Class has more dimensions than access to economic and social resources. It is a contested social position in a social space and a source of common identification; this social position is expressed by self-attributions of specific knowledge and experiences that are compared with those of others. The emotional efficacy of class has found its specific expressions in the workers' common narratives. In this sense, the interviewees' nostalgic narratives can be seen as class-related emotions that are actively expressing their current social position and contribute to a common class identity today.

This also explains why workers repeatedly visit their former workplaces (even if these are in ruins today) and why they actively confront themselves with an emotionally challenging and painful experience. The workers have developed a close relationship with their workplaces. By encountering these workplaces today, memories of better times are reactivated. These visits allow workers to cope with the loss, by reconstructing their class identity as workers through these shared emotional experiences.

The nostalgic narratives of the workers are understood in this book as idealisations of the past and expressions of a dissatisfaction with their present situation. This dissatisfaction with their current status became visible through their nostalgic considerations of a former life, seemingly in harmony and solidarity. This narrative was a specific perspective on their former powerful position in a city quarter, where the outsiders have had to adapt themselves under the rules of the powerful established. The loss of power within the established-outsider figuration came together with a change of perception. Now the former outsiders have become more powerful and more visible to the former established. This example stresses the troubles that accompany nostalgia. Rightly, Doreen Massey has formulated that:

> When nostalgia articulates space and time in such a way that it robs others of their histories (their stories), then indeed we need to rework nostalgia.
>
> (Massey 2005: 124)

Such a reworking has been achieved in this book by interpreting nostalgia as a powerful issue in the established-outsider figuration and by including the stories of others. The narratives of the former outsiders differ. Unlike the former established, the former outsider – who has experienced upward social mobility – does not express a nostalgic perspective on an idealised past. To understand this it is obviously necessary to employ an intersectional perspective. The former established are frustrated about their loss of power in the local figuration. The loss of power of the former established in this specific local setting of Nuremberg is entangled by the loss of symbolic capital that manual workers have experienced in general.

The nostalgic perspectives employed in the narratives were in some cases accompanied by a negative classification of others. Such an entanglement of loss of symbolic power (together with other aspects such as: a feeling of loss of political representation of interests, an increasingly precarious employment status, economic restructurings and a rise in social inequality, restricted social security through marketisation of welfare state benefits) has been analysed in studies explaining the rise of right-wing and racist parties.

The switch from a self-placement within class differences to self-placement in constructed differences between "ethnicities" is analysed in books by Didier Eribon (2009) in France, Andreas Reckwitz in Germany (2020) and Russell Hochschild (2016) in the USA.

Obviously, emotions reflect and express social positions in unequal societies but it remains to be established whether those emotions will be understood and contextualised as outcomes of class differentiations.

References

Adams, Matthew and Raisborough, Jayne (2008): What Can Sociology Say about Fair Trade? Class, Reflexivity and Ethnical Consumption; *Sociology* 42(6): 1165–1182.

Adams, Maurianne; Blumenfeld, Warren J.; Castañeda, Rosie; Hackman, Heather W.; Peters, Madeline L. and Zúñiga, Ximena (2000): *Readings for Diversity and Social Justice. An Anthology on Racism, Antisemitism, Sexism, Heterosexism, Ableism, and Classism*; New York: Routledge.

Ahmed, Sara (1999): Home and Away. Narratives of Migration and Estrangement; *International Journal of Cultural Studies* 2(3): 329–347.

Al-Ali, Nadje and Koser, Khalid (eds.) (2002): *New Approaches to Migration? Transnational Communities and the Transformation of Home*; London: Routledge.

Albert, Michel (1992): *Kapitalismus contra Kapitalismus*; Frankfurt a.M.: Campus Verlag.

Alexander, Jeffrey C. (2003): *The Meanings of Social Life. A Cultural Sociology*; Oxford: Oxford University Press.

Altay, Denis (2007): Urban Spaces Re-Defined in Daily Practices – 'Minibar', Ankara; In: Frers, Lars and Meier, Lars (eds.). *Encountering Urban Places. Visual and Material Performances in the City*. pp. 63–80. Aldershot: Ashgate.

Altenhain, Claudio; Danilina, Anja; Hildebrandt, Erik; Kausch, Stefan; Müller, Annekathrin and Roscher, Tobias (eds.) (2008): *Von 'Neuer Unterschicht' und Prekariat*; Bielefeld: Transcript.

Altman, Irwin and Low Setha M. (eds.) (1992): *Place Attachments*; Plenum Press: New York.

Amin, Ash (2012): *Land of Strangers*; Cambridge: Polity Press.

Anderson, Benedict (1983): *Imagined Communities*; London: Verso.

Anderson, Elijah (2011): *The Cosmopolitan Canopy: Race and Civility in Everyday Life*; New York: Norton.

Anderson, Kay and Smith, Susan J. (2001): Editorial: Emotional Geographies; *Transactions of the Institute of British Geographers* 26(1): 7–10.

Angé, Olivia and Berliner, David (eds.) (2015): *Anthropology and Nostalgia*; Oxford/New York: Berghahn.

Antonsich, Marco (2010): Searching for Belonging – An Analytical Framework; *Geography Compass* 4(6): 644–659.

Assmann, Aleida (2006): Memory, Individual and Collective; In: Goodin, Robert E. and Tilly, Charles (eds.). *The Oxford Handbook of Contextual Political Analysis*. pp. 210–224. Oxford: Oxford University Press.
Assmann, Jan (2005): *Religion and Cultural Memory: Ten Studies*; Stanford: Stanford University Press.
Atia, Nadia and Davies, Jeremy (2010): Nostalgia and the Shapes of History; *Memory Studies* 3(3): 181–186.
Atkinson, Will (2010): The Myth of the Reflexive Worker. Class and Work Histories in neo-liberal Times; *Work, Employment and Society* 24(3): 413–429.
Bach, Stefan; Thiemann, Andreas and Zucco, Aline (2018): Looking for the Missing Rich: Tracing the Top Tail of the Wealth Distribution; DIW Discussion Paper 1717. Berlin: DIW.
Back, Les (2009): Researching Community and its Moral Projects; *Twenty-First Century Society: Journal of the Academy of Social Sciences* 4(2): 201–214.
Baldassar, Loretta (2007): Transnational Families and the Provision of Moral and Emotional Support: The Relationship between Truth and Distance; *Identities* 14(4): 385–409.
Barthel, Diane (1996): Getting in Touch with History: The Role of Historic Preservation in Shaping Collective Memories; *Qualitative Sociology* 19(3): 345–364.
Barwick, Christine (2017): Are Immigrants Really Lacking Social Networking Skills? The Crucial Role of Reciprocity in Building Ethnically Diverse Networks; *Sociology* 51(2): 1–19.
Bauman, Zygmunt (1991): Modernity and Ambivalence; In: Mike Featherstone (ed.). *Global Culture. Nationalism, Globalization and Modernity*. pp. 143–169. London: Sage.
Bauman, Zygmunt (2005): *Work, Consumerism and the New Poor*; London: Open University Press.
Bauman, Zygmunt (2007): *Consuming Life*; Oxford: Polity Press.
Baur, Nina (2016): *Verlaufsmusteranalyse. Entwurf einer prozessorientierten Methodologie*, 2nd edition; Wiesbaden: VS-Verlag für Sozialwissenschaften.
Baur, Nina and Ernst, Stefanie (2011): Towards a Process-Oriented Methodology. Modern Social Science Research Methods and Nobert Elias' Figurational Sociology; *The Sociological Review* 59(1): 117–139.
Beck, Ulrich (1992): *Risk Society – Towards a New Modernity*; London: Sage.
Beck, Ulrich (1999): *What is Globalization?* Cambridge: Polity Press.
Beck, Ulrich (2000): *The Brave New World of Work*; Cambridge: Polity.
Beck, Ulrich (2002): The Cosmopolitan Society and its Enemies; *Theory, Culture & Society* 19(1–2): 17–44.
Beck, Ulrich (2007): Beyond Class and Nation. Reframing Social Inequalities in a Globalising World; *British Journal of Sociology* 58(4): 679–705.
Beck, Ulrich and Beck-Gernsheim, Elisabeth (2002): *Individualization*; London: Sage.
Beer, Helmut (2004): *Südstadtgeschichte. Aus der Vergangenheit der Nürnberger Südstadt*; Ausstellungskatalog des Stadtarchivs Nürnberg; Nürnberg: Edelmann.
Bell, Daniel (1974): *The Coming of Post-Industrial Society*; New York: Harper.
Bell, Michael M. (1997): The ghosts of place; *Theory and Society* 26: 813–836.
Benjamin, Walter (2006 [1938]): *Berlin Childhood around 1900*; Cambridge: Harvard University Press.

Benjamin, Walter (2008 [1936]): *The Work of Art in the Age of Its Technological Reproducibility, and Other Writings on Media*; Cambridge, MA: Belknap Press.
Berger, Peter L. and Luckmann, Thomas (1966): *The Social Construction of Reality: A Treatise in the Sociology of Knowledge*; New York: Doubleday.
Berking, Helmuth (2010): The Working Class in Capitalist Countries. Conceptual Traps and Political Opportunity Structures; In: Oommen, T.K. (ed.). *Classes, Citizenship and Inequality*. pp. 64–76. New Delhi: Pearson.
Berking, Helmuth and Löw, Martina (eds.) (2008): *Die Eigenlogik der Städte. Neue Wege für die Stadtforschung*; Frankfurt a.M.: Campus.
Berndt, Christian and Boeckler, Marc (2007): The City as a World-place: Transterritorial Flows and Territorial Order in a Nuremberg Neighbourhood; *Environment and Planning A* 39(7): 1545–1563.
Bhabha, Homi (1994): *The Location of Culture*; London: Routledge.
Blackshaw, Tony (2010): *Key Concepts in Community Studies*; London: Sage.
Blackshaw, Tony (2013): *Working-Class Life in Northern England, 1945–2010 – The Pre-History and After-Life of the Inbetweener Generation*; Basingstoke: Palgrave.
Blokland, Talja (2001): Bricks, Mortar, Memories: Neighbourhoods and Networks in Collective Acts of Remembering; *International Journal of Urban and Regional Research* 25(2): 268–283.
Blokland, Talja (2003): *Urban Bonds*; Cambridge: Polity Press.
Blunt, Alison and Dowling, Robyn (2006): *Home*; London: Routledge.
Boltanski, Luc and Chiapello, Ève (2003): *Der neue Geist des Kapitalismus*; Konstanz: UVK.
Bondi, Liz (2005): Making Connections and Thinking through Emotions: Between Geography and Psychotherapy; *Transactions of the Institute of British Geographers* 30(4): 433–448.
Borden, Iain (2001): *Skateboarding, Space and the City. Architecture and the Body*; Oxford: Berg.
Bourdieu, Pierre (1984 [1979]): *Distinction. A Social Critique of the Judgement of Taste*; Cambridge: Harvard University Press.
Bourdieu, Pierre (1990 [1980]): *The Logic of Practice*; Cambridge: Polity.
Bourdieu, Pierre (2004 [1986]): The Biographical Illusion; In: du Gay, Paul; Evans, Jessica and Redman, Peter (eds.). *Identity: A Reader*. pp. 297–303. London: Sage.
Bourdieu, Pierre (2008): *Sketch for a Self-Analysis*; Cambridge: Polity Press.
Boym, Svetlana (2001): *The Future of Nostalgia*. New York: Basic.
Bradley, Andrew; Hall, Tim and Harrison, Margaret (2002): Selling Cities. Promoting New Images for Meetings Tourism; *Cities* 19(1): 61–70.
Brah, Avtar (1996): *Cartographies of Diaspora: Contesting Identities*. London: Routledge.
Braun, Helmut (2007): Industrialisierung; In: *Historisches Lexikon Bayerns*. http://www.historisches-lexikon-bayerns.de/Lexikon/Industrialisierung (accessed 3.09.2019).
Braverman, Harry (1974): *Labour and Monopoly Capital. The Degradation of Work in the Twentieth Century*; London: Monthly Review Press.
Bridge, Gary and Watson, Sophie (2003): *A Companion to the City*; Chichester: Blackwell.
Bröckling, Ulrich (2016): *The Entrepreneurial Self*; London: Sage.
Brubaker, Rogers (2006): *Ethnicity without Groups*; Cambridge, MA: Harvard University Press.

Bryceson, Deborah Fahy and Vuorela, Ulla (2002): *The Transnational Family: New European Frontiers and Global Networks*; Oxford: Berg.

Buchanan, Ian (2000): *Michel de Certeau – Cultural Theorist*; London: Sage.

Bude, Heinz (1984): Rekonstruktion von Lebenskonstruktionen; In: Kohli, Martin and Robert, Günther (eds.). *Biographie und soziale Wirklichkeit*. pp. 7–28. Stuttgart: Metzler.

Bude, Heinz and Willisch, Andreas (eds.) (2007): *Exklusion. Die Debatte über die 'Überflüssigen'*; Frankfurt a.M.: Suhrkamp.

Bundesagentur für Arbeit (2018): *Die Arbeitsmarktsituation von Frauen und Männern 2017;* Blickpunkt Arbeitsmarkt Juli 2018; Nürnberg: Bundesagentur für Arbeit.

Bundesanstalt für Arbeitsschutz und Arbeitsmedizin (2018): *Arbeitswelt im Wandel. Zahlen-Daten-Fakten*; Dortmund: Bundesanstalt für Arbeitsschutz und Arbeitsmedizin (BAuA).

Butler, Judith (1993): *Bodies that Matter – On the discursive limits of „Sex"*; London: Routledge.

Butterwegge, Christoph (2006): *Krise und Zukunft des Sozialstaates*; Wiesbaden: VS.

Casey, Edward S. (1987): *Remembering. A Phenomenological Study*; Bloomington: Indiana University Press.

Castel, Robert (2000): *Die Metamorphosen der sozialen Frage. Eine Chronik der Lohnarbeit*; Konstanz: UVK.

Castel, Robert (2009): Die Wiederkehr der sozialen Unsicherheit; In: Dörre, Klaus and Castel, Robert (eds.). *Prekarität, Abstieg, Ausgrenzung. Die soziale Frage am Beginn des 21. Jahrhunderts*. pp. 21–34. Frankfurt a.M.: Campus Verlag.

Castells, Manuel (2010): *The Rise of the Network Society: The Information Age: Economy, Society, and Culture Volume I*, 2nd edition; Malden: Wiley-Blackwell.

Castles, Stephen and Davidson, Alastair (2000): *Citizenship and Migration. Globalization and the Politics of Belonging*; London: Routledge.

Chakrabarty, Dipesh (2000): *Rethinking Working-Class History. Bengal 1890–1940*; Princeton: Princeton University Press.

Chamberlain, Mary and Leydesdorff, Selma (2004): Transnational Families: Memories and Narratives; *Global Networks* 4(3): 227–241.

Charlesworth, Simon J. (2000): *A Phenomenology of Working Class Experience*; Cambridge: Cambridge University Press.

Charmaz, Kathy (2014): *Constructing Grounded Theory*, 2nd edition; London: Sage.

Chase, Malcolm and Shaw, Christopher (eds.) (1989): *The Imagined Past: History and Nostalgia*; Manchester: Manchester University Press.

Chassé, Karl August (2010): *Unterschichten in Deutschland. Materialien zu einer kritischen Debatte*; Wiesbaden: VS Verlag.

Chiu, Chihsin (2009): Contestation and Conformity. Street and Park Skateboarding in New York City Public Space; *Space and Culture* 12(1): 25–42.

Coddingtona, Kate S. (2011): Spectral Geographies: Haunting and Everyday State Practices in Colonial and Present-day Alaska; *Social & Cultural Geography* 12(7): 743–756.

Collis, Marion (2005): 'Mourning the Loss' or 'No Regrets'. Exploring Women's Emotional Responses to Hysterectomy; In: Davidson, Joyce; Bondi, Liz and Smith, Mick (eds.). *Emotional Geographies*. pp. 33–48. Aldershot: Ashgate.

Conway, Brian (2010): New Directions in the Sociology of Collective Memory and Commemoration; *Sociology Compass* 4(7): 442–453.

Crawford, Margaret (1995): *Building the Workingman's Paradise. The Design of American Company Towns*; London: Verso.

Crenshaw, Kimberlé (1989): Demarginalizing the Intersection of Race and Sex: A Black Feminist Critique of Antidiscrimination Doctrine; *The University of Chicago Legal Forum* 140: 139–167.

Crow, Graham and Allen, Graham (1994): *Community Life. An Introduction to Local Social Relations*; Hemel Hempstead: Harvester Wheatsheaf.

Daatland, Svein and Biggs, Simon (eds.) (2006): *Ageing and Diversity*; Bristol: Policy Press.

Davidson, Joyce; Liz Bondi and Mick Smith (eds.) (2005): *Emotional Geographies*; Aldershot: Ashgate.

Davidson, Tonya (2009): The Role of Domestic Architecture in the Structuring of Memory; *Space and Culture* 12(3): 332–342.

Davis, Fred (1979): *Yearning for Yesterday: A Sociology of Nostalgia*; New York: Macmillan.

Davis, Mike (1990): *City of Quartz. Excavating the Future in Los Angeles*; London: Verso.

de Certeau, Michel (1988 [1980]): *The Practice of Everyday Life*; Berkeley: University of California Press.

Decker, Oliver; Kiess, Johannes; Eggers, Eva and Brähler, Elmar (2016): Die Mitte Studie 2016. Methode, Ergebnisse, und Langzeitverlauf; In: Decker, Oliver; Kiess, Johannes and Brähler, Elmar (eds.). *Die enthemmte Mitte. Autoritäre und rechtsextreme Einstellung in Deutschland.* pp. 23–66. Gießen: Psychosozial Verlag.

Degnen, Cathrine (2005): Relationality, Place, and Absence. A Three-dimensional Perspective on Social Memory; *The Sociological Review* 53(4): 729–744.

DeLyser, Dydia (1999): Authenticity on the Ground. Engaging the Past in a California Ghost Town; *Annals of the American Geographers* 89(4): 602–632.

DeLyser Dydia (2003): „A walk through Old Bodie" Presenting a Ghost Town in a Tourism Map; In: Hanna, Stephen P. and Del Casino, Vincent J. (eds.). *Mapping Tourism*. pp. 79–106. Minneapolis: University of Minnesota Press.

DeLyser, Dydia (2001): When Less is More. Absence and Social Memory in a California Ghost Town; In: Adams, Paul C.; Hoelscher, Steven and Till, Karen E. (eds.). *Textures of Places. Exploring Humanist Geographies*. pp. 24–40. Minneapolis: University of Minnesota Press.

Dennis, Norman; Henriques, Fernando and Slaughter, Clifford (1956): *Coal is our Life. An Analysis of a Yorkshire Mining Community*; London: Tavistock.

Deppe, Frank (1971): *Das Bewusstsein der Arbeiter. Studien zur politischen Soziologie des Arbeiterbewusstseins*; Köln: Pahl-Rugenstein.

Der Spiegel (2000): Ein ungeheuer belastendes Klima; *Der Spiegel* 44: 144ff.

Derrida, Jacques (1994): *Specters of Marx: The State of the Debt, the Work of Mourning and the New International*; London: Routledge.

DeSilvey, Caitlin (2006): Observed Decay – Telling Stories with Mutable Things; *Journal of Material Culture* 11(3): 318–338.

DeSilvey, Caitlin (2012): Copper Places. Affective Circuitries; In: Jones, Owain and Garde-Hansen, Joanne (eds.). *Geography and Memory. Explorations in Identity, Place and Becoming*. pp. 45–57. Basingstoke: Palgrave Macmillan.

Dicks, Bella (2008): Performing the Hidden Injuries of Class in Coal-Mining Heritage; *Sociology* 42(3): 436–452.

Diefenbacher, Michael (2010): *Nürnberg, Reichsstadt: Handel*; In: Historisches Lexikon Bayerns. http://www.historisches-lexikon-bayerns.de/Lexikon/Nürnberg,_Reichsstadt:_Handel (accessed 3.09.2019).

Doherty, Michael (2009): When the Working Day is Through: The End of Work as Identity? *Work Employment & Society* 23(1): 84–101.

Dörre, Klaus; Happ, Anja and Matuschek, Ingo (2013): Das Unbehagen am Kapitalismus und die LohnarbeiterInnen; In: Dörre, Klaus; Happ, Anja and Matuschek, Ingo (eds.). *Das Gesellschaftsbild der LohnarbeiterInnen. Soziologische Untersuchungen in ost- und westdeutschen Industriebetrieben*. pp. 9–28. Hamburg: VSA Verlag.

Dörre, Klaus; Scherschel, Karin; Booth, Melanie; Haubner, Tine; Marquardsen Kai and Schierhorn, Karen (2013): *Bewährungsproben für die Unterschicht? Soziale Folgen aktivierender Arbeitsmarktpolitik*; Frankfurt a.M.: Campus Verlag.

Douglas, Mary (1966): *Purity and Danger: An Analysis of Concepts of Pollution and Taboo*; London: Routledge.

Duyvendak, Jan W. (2011). *The Politics of Home. Belonging and Nostalgia in Western Europe and the United States*; Basingstoke: Palgrave Macmillan.

Eade, John (1997): Reconstructing Places. Changing images of locality in Docklands and Spitalfield; In: Eade, John (ed.). *Living the Global City*. pp. 127–145. London: Routledge.

Eastmond, Marita (2007): Stories as Lived Experience: Narratives in Forced Migration Research; *Journal of Refugee Studies* 20(2): 248–264.

Edensor, Tim (2005a): *Industrial Ruins. Space, Aesthetics and Materiality*; Oxford: Berg.

Edensor, Tim (2005b): Waste Matters. The Debris of Industrial Ruins and the Disordering of the Material World; *Journal of Material Culture* 10(3): 311–332.

Edensor, Tim (2008): Mundane Hauntings: Commuting through the Phantasmagoric Working-class Spaces of Manchester, England; *Cultural Geographies* 15: 313–333.

Elfick, Jacqueline (2011): Class Formation and Consumption among Middle-Class Professionals in Shenzhen; *Journal of Current Chinese Affairs*; 40(1): 187–211.

Elias, Norbert (1984 [1907]): *What is Sociology?* New York: Columbia University Press.

Elias, Norbert (2001 [1987]): Changes in the We-I Balance; In: Elias, Norbert. *The Society of Individuals*; pp. 153–237; New York and London: Continuum.

Elias, Norbert and Scotson, John (1965): *The Established and the Outsiders. A Sociological Enquiry into Community Problems*; London: Frank Cass.

Elsley, Susan (2004): Children's Experience of Public Space; *Children & Society* 18(2): 155–164.

Elwood, Sarah A. and Martin, Deborah G. (2000): „Placing" Interviews: Location and Scales of Power in Qualitative Research; *Professional Geographer* 52(4): 649–657.

Engels, Friedrich (1845): *Die Lage der arbeitenden Klasse in England*; Leipzig: Verlag Otto Wigand.

Entrikin, J. Nicholas (1991): *The Betweenness of Place. Towards a Geography of Modernity*; Baltimore: John Hopkins University Press.

Eribon, Didier (2009): *Retour à Reims*; Paris: Librairie Artème Fayard.

Erikson, Robert and Goldthorpe, John H. (1992): *The Constant Flux. A Study of Class Mobility in Industrial Societies*; Oxford: Clarendon Press.

Erll, Astrid (2011): *Kollektives Gedächtnis und Erinnerungskulturen*; 2. Auflage. Stuttgart: J.B. Metzler.
Erll, Astrid and Nünning, Ansgar (eds.) (2008): *Cultural Memory Studies*; Berlin: de Gruyter.
Esping-Andersen, Gøsta (1990): *The Three Worlds of Welfare Capitalism*; Cambridge: Polity Press.
Espinoza, Adriana E.; Piper, Isabel and Fernández, Roberto A. (2014): The study of memory sites through a Dialogical Accompaniment Interactive Group Method: A Research Note; *Qualitative Research* 14(6): 712–728.
Eurostat (2019): Inequality of Income Distribution S80/S20 Income Quintile Share Ratio – EU-SILC survey [ilc_pns4]. http://appsso.eurostat.ec.europa.eu/nui/submitViewTableAction.do (accessed 07.02.2019).
Featherstone, Mike (1991): *Consumer Culture and Postmodernism*; London: Sage.
Fiske, John (1987): *Television Culture*; New York: Routledge.
Florida, Richard (2004): *The Rise of the Creative Class*; New York: Basic Books.
Florida, Richard (2005): *Cities and the Creative Class*; New York: Routledge.
Flyvbjerg, Bent (2006): Five Misunderstandings about Case-Study Research; *Qualitative Inquiry* 12(2): 219–245.
Fohrbeck, Anna; Hirseland, Andreas and Ramos Lobato, Philipp (2014): How Benefits Recipients Perceive Themselves through the Lens of the Mass Media – Some Observations from Germany; *Sociological Research Online* 19(4): 1–9.
Foster, Sarah; Villanueva, Karen; Wood, Lisa; Christian, Hayley and Giles-Corti, Billie (2014): The Impact of Parents' Fear of Strangers and Perceptions of Informal Social Control on Children's Independent Mobility; *Health & Place* 26: 60–68.
Foucault, Michel (1969): *L'archéologie du savoir*; Paris: Éditions Gallimard.
Foucault, Michel (1979 [1976]): *The History of Sexuality, Vol. 1*; London: Allen Lane.
Foucault, Michel (1991 [1975]): *Discipline and Punish. The Birth of the Prison*; London: Penguin.
Frank, Sybille (2016): *Wall Memorials and Heritage – The Heritage Industry of Berlin's Checkpoint Charlie*; London: Routledge.
Frank, Sybille; Schwenk, Jochen; Steets, Silke and Weidenhaus, Gunter (2013): Der aktuelle Perspektivenstreit in der Stadtsoziologie; *Leviathan* 41(2): 197–223.
Freestone, Robert (1989): *Model Communities. The Garden City Movement in Australia*; Melbourne: Nelson.
Frers, Lars (2013): The Matter of Absence; *Cultural Geographies* 20(4): 431–445.
Frers, Lars and Meier, Lars (eds.) (2007): *Encountering Urban Places – Visual and Material Performances in the City*; London: Routledge.
Frers, Lars and Meier, Lars (2021): Hierarchy and Inequality in Research: Practices, Ethics and Experiences; Special Issue. *Qualitative Research* (in prep.).
Fröbel, Folker; Heinrichs, Jürgen and Kreye, Otto (1980): The New International Division of Labour. Cambridge: Cambridge University Press.
Frick, Joachim R. and Grabka, Markus M. (2009): Zur Entwicklung der Vermögensungleichheit in Deutschland; *Berliner Journal für Soziologie* 19(4): 577–600.
Frisby, David (2007): *Cityscapes of Modernity*; Cambridge: Polity.
Fuchs, Michaela (2018): *Regionale Lohnunterschiede zwischen Männern und Frauen in Deutschland*; Aktuelle Daten und Indikatoren 12.2.2018. Institut für Arbeitsmarkt und Berufsforschung, Nürnberg.
Gans, Herbert J. (1962): *The Urban Villagers. Group and Class in the Life of Italian Americans*; New York: The Free Press.

Gardner, Katy (2002): *Narrative, Age and Migration*; Oxford: Berg.

Garske, Pia (2013): Intersektionalität als Herrschaftskritik? Die Kategorie ‚Klasse' und das gesellschaftskritische Potenzial der Intersektionalitätsdebatte; In: Kallenberg, Vera; Meyer, Jennifer and Müller, Johanna M. (eds.). *Intersectionality und Kritik*. pp. 245–263. Wiesbaden: VS Springer.

Geißler, Rainer (2011): *Die Sozialstruktur Deutschlands*, 6th edition; Wiesbaden: VS Verlag.

Gerhards, Jürgen (1988): *Soziologie der Emotionen – Fragestellung, Systematik und Perspektiven*; Weinheim: Juventa.

Giddens, Anthony (1988): *Die Konstitution der Gesellschaft – Grundzüge einer Theorie der Strukturierung*; Frankfurt a.M.: Campus.

Giddens, Anthony (1990): *The Consequences of Modernity*; Stanford: Stanford University Press.

Giddens, Anthony (1994): Living in Post-traditional Society; In: Beck, Ulrich; Giddens, Anthony and Lash, Scott (eds.). *Reflexive Modernization. Politics, Tradition and Aesthetics in the Modern Social Order*. pp. 56–108. Cambridge: Polity Press.

Gidley, Ben and Rooke, Alison (2010): Asdatown: The Intersections of Classed Places and Identities; In: Taylor, Yvette (ed.). *Classed Intersections: Spaces, Selves, Knowledges*. pp. 95–115. London: Ashgate.

Giebeler, Cornelia; Rademacher, Claudia and Schulze, Erika (2013): *Intersektionen von Race, Class, Gender, Body*; Opladen, Berlin & Toronto: Barbara Budrich Verlag.

Gill, Nick (2010). Pathologies of Migrant Place-making. The Case of Polish Migrants to the UK; *Environment and Planning A* 42: 1157–1173.

Gilloch, Graeme (1996): *Myth and Metropolis: Walter Benjamin and the City*; Cambridge: Polity.

Gilroy, Paul (2005): *Postcolonial Melancholia*; New York: Columbia University Press.

Goebel, Jan; Grabka, Markus M. and Schröder, Carsten (2015): Einkommensungleichheit in Deutschland bleibt weiterhin hoch – Junge Alleinlebende und Berufseinsteiger sind zunehmend von Armut bedroht; *DIW Wochenbericht* 25.

Goffman, Erving (1977): *Rahmen-Analyse. Ein Versuch über die Organisation von Alltagserfahrungen*; Frankfurt a.M.: Suhrkamp.

Goldthorpe, John H. (1996): Class Analysis and the Reorientation of Class Theory; *British Journal of Sociology* 47(3): 481–505.

Gordon, Avery F. (2008): *Ghostly Matters: Haunting and the Sociological Imagination*, 2nd edition; Minneapolis: University of Minnesota Press.

Gorz, André (1999): *Reclaiming Work: Beyond the Wage-Based Society*; Cambridge: Cambridge University Press.

Grabka, Markus and Frick, Joachim (2008): Schrumpfende Mittelschicht – Anzeichen einer dauerhaften Polarisierung der verfügbaren Einkommen? *DIW-Wochenbericht* 8.

Grabka, Markus and Westermeier, Christian (2014): Anhaltend hohe Vermögensungleichheit in Deutschland; *DIW Wochenbericht* 9: 151–164.

Graham, Brian J.; Ashworth, Gregory John and Tunbridge, J.E. (2000): *A Geography of Heritage. Power, Culture and Economy*; London: Routledge.

Groh-Samberg, Olaf (2004): Armut und Klassenstruktur. Zur Kritik der Entgrenzungsthese aus einer multidimensionalen Perspektive; *Kölner Zeitschrift für Soziologie und Sozialpsychologie* 56(4): 653–682.

Groh-Samberg, Olaf (2008): *Armut, soziale Ausgrenzung und Klassenstruktur*; Wiesbaden: VS Verlag.

Gross, Peter and Bertschi, Stefan (2006): Loading Mobile Phones in a Multi-option Society; *Knowledge, Technology & Policy* 19: 72–79.

Gustafson, Per (2001): Retirement Migration and Transnational Life Styles; *Ageing & Society* 21(4): 371–394.

Habermas, Jürgen (1991 [1962]): *The Structural Transformation of the Public Sphere. An Inquiry into a Category of Bourgeois Society*; Cambridge: MIT Press.

Hachtmann, Rüdiger (1993): Industriearbeiterinnen in der deutschen Kriegswirtschaft 1936 bis 1944/45; *Geschichte und Gesellschaft* 19: 332–366.

Hacking, Ian (1995): *Rewriting the Soul. Multiple Personality and the Science of Memory*; Princeton: Princeton University Press.

Haffner, Sebastian (1981): *Anmerkungen zu Hitler*; Frankfurt a.M.: Fischer Taschenbuch Verlag.

Halbwachs, Maurice (1980 [1950]): *The Collective Memory*; New York: Harper & Row.

Halbwachs, Maurice (1992 [1941]): *On Collective Memory*; Chicago: University of Chicago Press.

Hall, Stuart (ed.) (1997): *Representation. Cultural Representations and Signifying Practices*; London: Sage.

Hall, Stuart (1999): Old and new Identities; In: Black, Les and Solomos, John (eds.). *Theories of Race and Racism. A Reader*. pp. 144–153. London: Blackwell.

Hardy, Dennis (2000): *Utopian England. Community Experiments 1900–1945*; London: F.N. Spon.

Harvey, David (1990): *The Condition of Postmodernity*; Oxford: Blackwell.

Hayden, Dolores (1995): *The Power of Place. Urban Landscapes as Public History*; Cambridge, MA: MIT Press.

Herbst, Ludolf (1982): *Der totale Krieg und die Ordnung der Wirtschaft. Die Kriegswirtschaft im Spannungsfeld von Politik, Ideologie und Propaganda 1939–1945*; Stuttgart: Deutsche Verlagsanstalt Anstalt.

Hernandez, Bernardo; Hidalgo, M. Carmen; Salazar-Laplace, M. Esther and Hess, Stephany (2007): Place Attachment and Place Identity in Natives and Non-natives; *Journal of Environmental Psychology* 27: 310–319.

Hetherington Kevin and Degen, Monica (2001): Special Issue: Spatial Hauntings; *Space and Culture* 1(11/12).

Hewison Robert (1987): *The Heritage Industry: Britain in a Climate of Decline*; Methuen, London.

High, Steven and Lewis, David W. (2007): *Corporate Wasteland. The Landscape and Memory of Deindustrialisation*; New York: Cornell University Press.

Hirsch, Joachim and Roth, Roland (1986): *Das neue Gesicht des Kapitalismus. Vom Fordismus zum Post-Fordismus*; Hamburg: VSA Verlag.

Hitzler, Ronald (2003): Die Bastelgesellschaft; In: Prisching, Manfred (ed.). *Modelle der Gegenwartsgesellschaft*. pp. 65–80. Wien: Passagen.

Hitzler, Ronald and Honer, Anne (1994): Bastelexistenz. Über subjektive Konsequenzen der Individualisierung; In: Beck, Ulrich and Beck-Gernsheim, Elisabeth (eds.). *Riskante Freiheiten*. pp. 307–315. Frankfurt a.M.: Suhrkamp.

Hobsbawm, Eric (1998): *Das Zeitalter der Extreme. Weltgeschichte des 20. Jahrhunderts*; München: DTV.

Hoelscher, Steven and Alderman, Derek H. (2004): Memory and Place: Geographies of a Critical Relationship; *Social and Cultural Geography* 5(3): 347–355.

Hoffmann, Elke and Romeu Gordo, Laura (2016): Lebenssituation älterer Menschen mit Migrationshintergrund (Kap. 2.3); In: Statistisches Bundesamt (Destatis), Wissenschaftszentrum Berlin für Sozialforschung (WZB), Sozio-oekonomisches Panel (SOEP) (ed.). *Datenreport 2016. Ein Sozialbericht für die Bundesrepublik Deutschland*. pp. 64–73. Bonn: Bundeszentrale für politische Bildung.

Hogenstijn, Maarten; Van Middelkoop, Daniël and Terlouw, Kees (2008): The Established, the Outsiders and Scale Strategies. Studying Local Power Conflicts; *The Sociological Review* 56(1): 144–161.

Honneth, Axel (1993): Die Wiederkehr der Armut; *Merkur* 47: 518–524.

Honneth, Axel (1996 [1992]): *Struggle for Recognition: The Moral Grammar of Social Conflicts*; Cambridge: Polity.

hooks, bell (2000): *Where We Stand – Class Matters*; New York: Routledge.

Hospers, Gert-Jan (2002): Industrial Heritage Tourism and Regional Restructuring in the European Union; *European Planning Studies* 10(3): 397–404.

Hubbard, Phil and Hall, Tim (eds.) (1998): *The Entrepreneurial City: Geographies of Politics, Regime and Representation*; Chichester: John Wiley and Sons.

Hunt, Alan (2012): The Civilisation Process and Emotional Life – The Intensification and Hollowing Out of Contemporary Emotions; In: Spencer, Dale; Walby, Kevin and Hunt, Alan (eds.). *Emotions Matter. A Relational Approach to Emotions*. pp. 137–160. Toronto: University of Toronto Press.

Jacobs, Jane (1992 [1961]) *The Death and Life of Great American Cities*; New York: Vintage Books.

Jameson, Frederic (1992 [1989]): *Postmodernism, or, the Cultural Logic of Late Capitalism*; Durham: Duke University Press.

Jessop, Bob (1995): The Regulation Approach, Governance and Post-Fordism: Alternative Perspectives on Economic and Political Change? *Economy and Society* 24(3): 307–333.

Johnson, Nuala C. (2003): *Ireland, the Great War and the Geography of Remembrance*; Cambridge: Cambridge University Press.

Jones, Owain (2000): Melting Geography: Purity, Disorder, Childhood and Space; In: Holloway, Sarah L. and Valentine, Gill (eds.). *Children's Geographies: Playing, Living, Learning*. London: Routledge.

Jones, Owain (2005): An Ecology of Emotion, Memory, Self and Landscape; In: Joyce Davidson; Bondi, Liz and Smith, Mick (eds.). *Emotional Geographies*. pp. 205–218. Aldershot: Ashgate.

Jones, Owain and Garde-Hansen, Joanne (eds.) (2012): *Geography and Memory. Explorations in Identity, Place and Becoming*; Basingstoke: Palgrave.

Jones, Owen (2011): *Chavs – The Demonization of the Working Class*; London: Verso.

Kazmierska, Kaja (2003): Migration Experiences and Changes of Identity. The Analysis of a Narrative; *Forum Qualitative Social Research* 4(3): Art. 21.

Kearns, Gerard and Chris, Philo (eds.) (1993*): Selling Places. The City as Cultural Capital, Past and Presence*; Oxford: Pergamon.

Kelly, Philip F. (2012): Migration, Transnationalism, and the Spaces of Class Identity; *PSHEV* 60(2): 153–186.

Kemper, Theodore (1978): *A Social Interactionist Theory of Emotions*; New York: John Wiley.

Kenyon, Gary; Bohlmeijer, Ernst and Randall, William L. (2010): *Storying Later Life*; Oxford: Oxford University Press.

Kern, Horst and Schumann, Michael (1970): *Industriearbeit und Arbeiterbewusstsein*; Teil I + II, Frankfurt a.M.: Europäische Verlagsanstalt.

Kern, Horst and Schumann, Michael (1984): *Das Ende der Arbeitsteilung?* München: C. H. Beck.

Kirk, John (2007): *Class, Culture and Social Change. On the Trail of the Working Class*; Basingstoke: Palgrave Macmillan.

Kirk, John (with Jefferys, Steve and Wall, Christine) (2012): Representing Identity and Work in Transition. The Case of South Yorkshire Coal-mining Communities in the UK; In: Kirk, John; Jefferys, Steve and Contrepois, Sylvie (eds.). *Changing Work and Community Identities in European Regions: Perspectives on the Past and Present*. pp. 184–216. Basingstoke: Palgrave.

Kirk, John; Contrepois, Sylvie and Jefferys, Steve (eds.) (2012): *Changing Work and Community Identities in European Regions. Perspectives on the Past and Present; Basingstoke*: Palgrave.

Kirk, John and Wall, Christine (2011): *Work and Identity. Historical and Cultural Contexts*; Basingstoke: Palgrave Macmillan.

Kirshenblatt-Gimblett, Barbara (1998): *Destination Culture. Tourism, Museums, and Heritage;* Berkeley, Los Angeles and London: University of California Press.

Klumpp-Leonard, Olaf (2007): Schub für die Südstadt – Sieben Jahre Geld von Europa; In: Baumann, Wolfgang; Diefenbacher, Michael; Herbers, Hiltrud; Krüger, Fred and Wiktorin, Dorothea (eds.). *Der Nürnberg Atlas*. pp. 106–107. Nürnberg: Emons Verlag.

Knoblauch, Hubert (2005): Focused Ethnography; *Forum: Qualitative Social Research* 6(3): Art. 44.

Kofman, Eleonore (2008): Stratifikation und aktuelle Migrationsbewegungen. Überlegungen zu Geschlechterverhältnis und Klassenzugehörigkeit; In: Berger, Peter A. and Weiß, Anja (eds.). *Transnationalisierung sozialer Ungleichheit*; pp. 107–134. Wiesbaden: VS Springer.

Kolb, Patricia (2014): *Understanding Aging and Diversity*; London: Routledge.

Koppetsch, Cornelia (2013): *Die Wiederkehr der Konformität. Streifzüge durch die gefährdete Mitte*; Frankfurt a.M.: Campus.

Kraemer, Klaus (2014): Prekarisierung; *Soziologische Revue* 37: 437–444.

Krapf, Manfred (2013): Urbanisierung; In: *Historisches Lexikon Bayerns*. http://www.historisches-lexikon-bayerns.de/Lexikon/Urbanisierung (accessed 4.09.2019).

Kristeva, Julia (1982 [1980]): *The Powers of Horror – An Essay on Abjection*; New York: Columbia University Press.

Kristeva, Julia (1991 [1988]): *Strangers to Ourselves*; New York: Columbia University Press.

Kronauer, Martin (2010): *Exklusion. Die Gefährdung des Sozialen im hoch entwickelten Kapitalismus*, 2nd edition; Frankfurt a.M.: Campus.

Kudera, Werner; Ruff, Konrad and Schmidt, Rudi (1982): Soziale Lage und Bewußtsein von Arbeitern; In: Littek, Wolfgang; Rammert, Werner and Wachtler, Günther (eds.). *Einführung in die Arbeits- und Industriesoziologie*. pp. 269–283; Frankfurt a.M.: Campus.

Lange, Helmuth and Meier, Lars (eds.) (2009): *The New Middle Classes. Globalizing Lifestyles, Consumerism and Environmental Concern*; Dordrecht: Springer.

Lawler, Steph (2008): Stories and the Social World; In: Pickering, Michael (ed.). *Research Methods for Cultural Studies*. pp. 32–51. Edinburgh: Edinburgh University Press.

Le Roux, Brigitte; Rouanet, Henry; Savage, Mike and Warde, Alan (2008): Class and Cultural Divide in the UK; *Sociology* 42(6): 1049–1071.

Lee, Jo and Ingold, Timothy (2006): Fieldwork on Foot: Perceiving, Routing, Socializing; In: Coleman, Simon and Collins, Peter (eds.). *Locating the Field. Space, Place and Context in Anthropology*. pp. 67–86. Oxford: Berg.

Lees, Loretta; Slater, Tom and Wyly, Elvin K. (2010): *The Gentrification Reader*; London: Routledge.

Leitner, Helga (2012): Spaces of Encounters: Immigration, Race, Class, and the Politics of Belonging in Small-Town America; *Annals of the Association of American Geographers* 102(4): 828–846.

Lessenich, Stephan (2008): *Die Neuerfindung des Sozialen – Der Sozialstaat im flexiblen Kapitalismus*; Bielefeld: Transcript.

Lewis, Oscar (1966): *La Vida. A Puerto Rican Family in the Culture of Poverty*; New York: Random House.

Liggett, Helen (2003): *Urban Encounters*; Minneapolis: University of Minnesota Press.

Lipietz, Alain (1992): *Towards a New Economic Order: Post-Fordism, Democracy and Ecology*; Cambridge: Polity.

Lipietz, Alain (1998): *Nach dem Ende des „Goldenen Zeitalters". Regulation und Transformation kapitalistischer Gesellschaften*; Hamburg: Argument Verlag.

Lofland, Lyn (1973): *A World of Strangers. Order and Action in Urban Public Space*; Prospect Heights: Waveland Press.

Lohr, Karin and Nickel, Hildegard (eds.) (2009): *Subjektivierung von Arbeit. Riskante Chancen*; Münster: Westfälisches Dampfboot.

Lott, Yvonne (2019): *Weniger Arbeit mehr Freizeit?* WSI Report 47, Düsseldorf.

Löw, Martina (2008): *Soziologie der Städte*; Frankfurt a.M.: Suhrkamp.

Löw, Martina (2016): *The Sociology of Space. Materiality, Social Structures, and Action*; Basingstoke: Palgrave Macmillan.

Low, Setha (1996): Spatializing Culture. The Social Production and Social Construction of Public Space in Costa Rica; *American Ethnologis* 23(4): 861–879.

Low, Setha; Taplin, Dana and Scheld, Suzanne (2005): *Rethinking Urban Parks – Public Space and Cultural Diversity*; Austin: University of Texas Press.

Lowenthal, David (1985): *The Past is a Foreign Country*; Cambridge: Cambridge University Press.

Loyal, Steven (2011): A Land of Hundred Thousand Welcomes? Understanding Established and Outsiders Relations in Ireland; *The Sociological Review* 59: 181–201.

Lupton, Deborah (1999): Dangerous Places and the Unpredictable Stranger: Constructions of Fear of Crime; *The Australian and New Zealand Journal of Criminology* 32(1): 1–15.

Lutz, Burkart (1989): *Der kurze Traum immerwährender Prosperität: Eine Neuinterpretation der industriell-kapitalistischen Entwicklung im Europa des 20. Jahrhunderts*; Frankfurt a.M.: Campus.

Lutz, Helma; Herrera Vivar, Maria Teresa; Supik, Linda (2013): *Fokus Intersektionalität*; 2. Auflage; Wiesbaden: Springer VS.

MacKenzie, Robert; Stuart, Mark; Forde, Chris; Greenwood, Ian; Perrett, Robert and Gardiner, Jean (2005): All that is Solid Melts into Air. Class, Identity and the Maintance of a Collective Orientation Amongst Redundant Steelworkers; *Sociology* 40(5): 833–853.

Maddern, Jo Frances (2008): Spectres of Migration and the Ghost of Ellis Island; *Cultural Geographies* 15: 359–381.

Maddern, Jo Frances and Adey, Peter (2008): Special Issue on Spectro-Geographies; *Cultural Geographies* 15: 291–393.

Mah, Alice (2010): Memory, Uncertainty and Industrial Ruination: Walker Riverside, Newcastle upon Tyre; *International Journal of Urban and Regional Research* 34(2): 398–413.

Mah, Alice (2012): *Industrial Ruination, Community, and Place. Landscapes and Legacies of Urban Decline*; Toronto: University of Toronto Press.

Mannheim, Karl (1952 [1923]): The Sociological Problems of Generations; In: Kecskemeti, Paul (ed.). *Essays on the Sociology of Knowledge*. pp. 286–320. London: Routledge.

Marx, Karl (1847): *Das Elend der Philosophie*; Berlin: Dietz Verlag.

Marx, Karl and Friedrich Engels (1970 [1845/1846]): *The German Ideology*; London: Lawrance & Wishart.

Massey, Doreen (1995): The Conceptualisation of Place; In: Massey, Doreen and Jess, Patt (eds.). *A Place in the World? Places, Cultures and Globalisation*. pp. 45–86. Oxford: Oxford University Press.

Massey, Doreen (2005): *For Space*; London: Sage.

Massumi, Brian (1987): Notes on the Translation and Acknowledgements; In: Deleuze, Gilles and Guattari, Felix (eds.). *A Thousand Plateaus*. pp. ix–xx. Minneapolis: University of Minnesota Press.

Meier, Lars (2013a): Encounters with Haunted Industrial Workplaces and Emotions of Loss – Class Related Senses of Place within the Memories of Metalworkers; *Cultural Geographies* 20(4): 467–483.

Meier, Lars (2013b): Everyone Knew Everyone: Diversity, Community Memory and a New Established Outsider Figuration; *Identities* 20(4): 455–470.

Meier, Lars (ed.) (2015): *Migrant Professionals in the City. Local Encounters, Identities and Inequalities*; New York: Routledge.

Meier, Lars (2016a): Metalworkers' Nostalgic Memories and Optimistic Official Representations of a Transformed Industrial Landscape; *The Sociological Review* 64(4): 766–785.

Meier, Lars (2016b): „I Am Now a Nobody" – Transformations of Home and Senses of Belonging in the Life Narrative of a Migrant Worker in the Industrial Sector in Nuremberg; In: Walsh, Katie and Näre, Lena (eds.). *Transnational Migration and Home in Older Age*. pp. 165–175. New York: Routledge.

Meier, Lars (2017): Transformations of Public Space and the Limits of Resistance in Biographic Narratives of Workers. *Space and Culture* 20(2): 156–169.

Meier, Lars and Aytekin, Attila (2019): Transformed Landscapes and a Transnational Identity of Class: Narratives on (Post-)industrial Landscapes in Europe; *International Sociology* 34(1): 99–116.

Meier, Lars; Frers, Lars and Sigvardsdotter, Erika (2013): The Importance of Absence in the Present. Practices of Remembrance and the Contestation of Absences; *Cultural Geographies* 20(4): 423–430.

Meier, Lars and Promberger, Markus (2012): Industrial, Urban and Worker Identity Transitions in Nuremberg; In: Kirk, John; Jefferys, Steve and Contrepois, Sylvie (eds.). *Changing Work and Community Identities in European Regions: Perspectives on the Past and Present.* pp. 23–56. Basingstoke: Palgrave Macmillan.

Meine, Hartmut (2005): Arbeiter und Angestellte: Vom Ende und Beharrungsvermögen alter Scheidelinien; *WSI Mitteilungen* 2: 76–81.

Merleau-Ponty, Maurice (1962 [1945]): *Phenomenology of Perception*; London: Routledge.

Meusburger, Peter; Heffernan, Michael and Wunder, Edgar (eds.) (2011): *Cultural Memories. The Geographical Point of View*; Dordrecht: Springer.

Mieg, Harald and Oevermann, Heike (eds.) (2014): *Industrial Heritage Sites in Transformation – Clash of Discourses*; London: Routledge.

Miller, Robert L. (2000): *Researching Life Stories and Family Histories*; London: Sage.

Millington, Nate (2013): Post-industrial imaginaries. Nature, Representation and Ruin in Detroit; *International Journal of Urban and Regional Research* 37(1): 279–296.

Mills, Amy (2010): *Streets of Memory. Landscape, Tolerance, and National Identity in Istanbul*; Athens and London: The University of Georgia Press.

Misztal, Barbara A. (2003): *Theories of Social Remembering*; London: Open University Press.

Mitchell, Donald (1998): *Cultural Geography. A Critical Introduction*; Oxford: Blackwell.

Mitchell, Donald (2003): California living, California dying. Dead labor and the political economy of landscape; In: Anderson, Kay; Domosh, Mona; Pile, Steve and Thrift, Nigel (eds.). *Handbook of Cultural Geography.* pp. 233–248. London: Sage.

Mitchell, John P. (2007): A Fourth Critic of the Enlightenment: Michel de Certeau and the Ethnography of Subjectivity; *Social Anthropology/Anthropologie Sociale* 15(1): 89–106.

Moles, Kate (2008): A Walk in Thirdspace: Place, Methods and Walking. *Sociological Research Online*, 13(4): 31–39.

Mollona, Massimiliano (2009): *Made in Sheffield. An Ethnogrphy of Industrial Work and Politics*; Oxford: Berghahn.

Mooser, Josef (1984): *Arbeiterleben in Deutschland 1900–1970 – Klassenlagen, Kultur und Politik.* Frankfurt a.M.: Suhrkamp.

Morgan, David L. (1996): Focus Groups; *Annual Review of Sociology* 22: 129–152.

Morrissey, Belinda (2012): A Domestic Geography of Everyday Terror. Rembering and Forgetting the House I Grow Up In; In: Jones, Owain and Garde-Hansen, Joanne (eds.). *Geography and Memory. Explorations in Identitiy, Place and Becoming.* pp. 184–198. Basingstoke: Palgrave.

Museum Industriekultur (2013a): http://www.museen.nuernberg.de/industriekultur/index.html (accessed 7.6.2013).

Museum Industriekultur (2013b): http://www.museen.nuernberg.de/industriekultur/themen/museumsstrasse.html (accessed 7.6.2013).

Neckel, Sighard (1991): *Status und Scham. Zur symbolischen Reproduktion sozialer Ungleichheit*; Frankfurt a.M.: Campus Verlag.

Nora, Pierre (1989): Between Memory and History. Les lieux de mèmoire; *Representations* 26: 7–25.

Nora, Pierre (1996): *Realms of Memory. Rethinking the French Past*; New York: Columbia University Press.
O'Connor, Henrietta and Goodwin, John (2012): Revisiting Norbert Elias's Sociology of Community: Learning from the Leicester Re-Studies; *Sociological Review* 60(3): 476–497.
OECD (2020): Poverty Rate (indicator). doi:10.1787/0fe1315d-en (18.6.2020)
Olick, Jeffrey (2008): From Collective Memory to the Sociology of Mnemonic Practices and Products; In: Erll, Astrid and Nünning, Ansgar (eds.). *Cultural Memory Studies – An International and Interdisciplinary Handbook*. pp. 151–161. Berlin: de Gruyter.
Olick, Jeffrey and Robbins, Joyce (1998): Social Memory Studies: From „Collective Memory" to the Historical Sociology of Mnemonic Practices; *Annual Review of Sociology* 24: 105–140.
Oliver, Kelly (1993): *Reading Kristeva. Unraveling the Double-Blind*; Bloomington: Indiana University Press.
Paddison, Ronan (1993): City Marketing, Image Reconstruction and Urban Regeneration; *Urban Studies* 30: 339–349.
Pakulski, Jan and Waters, Malcom (1996): *The Death of Class*; London: Sage.
Parrenas, Rhacel S. (2005): *Children of Global Migration: Transnational Families and Gendered Woes*. Stanford: Stanford University Press.
Peacock, James and Holland, Dorothy (1993): The Narrated Self. Life Stories in Process; *Ethos* 21(4): 367–383.
Peck, Jamie (2005): Struggling with the Creative Class; *International Journal of Urban and Regional Research* 29(4): 740–770.
Phillipson, Chris (2007): The 'Elected' and the 'Excluded'. Sociological Perspectives on the Experience of Place and Community in Older Age; *Ageing & Society*: 321–342.
Phoenix, Ann (2006): Editorial. Intersectionality; *European Journal of Women's Studies* 13(3): 187–192.
Piketty, Thomas (2014): *Das Kapital im 21. Jahrhundert*; München: C.H.Beck.
Pile, Steve (2005): *Real Cities*; London: Sage.
Pile, Steve (2010): Emotions and Affect in Recent Human Geography; *Transactions of the Institute of British Geographers* 35(1): 5–20.
Pongratz, Hans and Voss, Günther (2003): *Arbeitskraftunternehmer. Erwerbsorientierung in entgrenzten Arbeitsformen*; Berlin: Edition Sigma.
Popitz, Heinrich; Bahrdt, Hans Paul; Jüres, Ernst August and Kesting, Hanno (1957): *Das Gesellschaftsbild des Arbeiters. Soziologische Untersuchungen in der Hüttenindustrie*; Tübingen: Mohr.
Przyborski, Aglaja and Wohlrab-Sahr, Monika (2010): *Qualitative Sozialforschung*; München: Oldenbourg.
Pusca, Anca (2010): Industrial and Human Ruins of Postcommunist Europe; *Space and Culture* 13(3): 239–255.
Ramji, Hasmita (2006): British Indians 'Returning Home'. An Exploration of Transnational Belongings; *Sociology* 40(4): 645–662.
Ransome, Paul (2005): *Work, Consumption & Culture. Affluence and Social Change in the Twenty-First Century*; London: Sage.
Reay, Diane (2005): Beyond Consciousness? The Psychic Landscape of Social Class; *Sociology* 39(5): 911–928.
Reckwitz, Andreas (2020): *Society of Singularities*; Cambridge: Polity Press.

Reid, Ivan (1998): *Class in Britain*; Cambridge: Polity Press.

Relph, Edward (1976): *Place and Placelessness*; London: Pion.

Revilla, Juan Carlos; Jefferys, Steve and Tovar Martínez, José (2013): Collective Identities in the Age of Restructuring: Old and New Class, Space and Community-based Identities in Six European Regions; *International Sociology* 28(4): 391–408.

Ricoeur, Paul (1991): Narrative Identity; In: Woods, David (ed.). *On Paul Ricoeur. Narrative and Interpretation.* pp. 188–199. London: Routledge.

Rifkin, Jeremy (1995): *The End of Work: The Decline of the Global Labor Force and the Dawn of the Post-Market Era*; New York: G.P. Putnam's Sons,

Robertson, Iain J.M. (2008): Heritage from Below. Class, Social Protest and Resistance; In: Graham, Brian and Howard, Peter (eds.). *The Ashgate Research Companion to Heritage and Identity*; pp. 144–158. Aldershot: Ashgate.

Robison, Richard and Goodman, David S.G. (eds.) (1996): *The New Rich in Asia. Mobile Phones, McDonalds and Middle Class Revolution*; London: Routledge.

Rogaly, Ben and Taylor, Becky (2009): *Moving Histories of Class and Community. Identity, Place and Belonging in Contemporary England*; Basingstoke: Palgrave Macmillan.

Rosa, Hartmut (2013): *Social Acceleration*; New York: Columbia University Press.

Rose, Gillian (1995): Place and Identity. A Sense of Place; In: Massey, Doreen and Jess, Pat (eds.). *A Place in the World? Places, Cultures and Globalisation.* pp. 87–132. Oxford: Oxford University Press.

Rosenthal, Gabriele (2004): Biographical Research; In: Gobo, Giampietro; Gubrium, Javier F.; Seale, Clive and Silverman, David (eds.). *Qualitative Research Practice.* pp. 48–64. London: Sage.

Rubinstein, Robert and Parmalee, Patricia (1992): Attachment to Place and the Representation of the Life Course by the Elderly; In: Altman, Irwin and Low, Sehta (eds.). *Place Attachment.* pp. 139–163. New York: Plenum Press.

Russell Hochschild, Arlie (2016): *Strangers in their Own Land. Anger and Mourning on the American Right*; New York: New Press.

Russo, John and Linkon, Lee Sherry (eds.) (2005): *New Working-Class Studies*; Ithaca and London: ILR Press.

Said, Edward (1999): *Out of Place*; New York: Alfred Knopf.

Salazar Parreñas, Rhacel (2008): Transnational Fathering: Gendered Conflicts, Distant Disciplining and Emotional Gaps; *Journal of Ethnic and Migration Studies* 34(7): 1057–1072.

Savage, Mike (2000): *Class Analysis and Social Transformation*; Buckingham: Open University Press.

Savage, Mike (2005): Working Class Identities in the 1960s – Revisiting the Affluent Worker Studies; *Sociology* 39(5): 929–946.

Savage, Mike (2014): Cultural Capital and Elective Belonging. A British Case Study; In: Thomä, Dieter; Henning, Christoph and Schmid, Hans Bernhard (eds.). *Social Capital, Social Identities.* pp. 29–53. Berlin: Walter de Gruyter.

Sayer, Andrew (2005): *The Moral Significance of Class*; Cambridge: Cambridge University Press.

Scharff, Christina (2008): Doing Class: A Discursive and Ethnomethodological Approach; *Critical Discourse Studies* 5(4): 331–343.

Schumann, Michael (1999): Das Lohnarbeiterbewußtsein des Arbeitskraftunternehmers; *SOFI-Mitteilungen* 27: 59–63.

Schumann, Michael (2000): Industriearbeit zwischen Entfremdung und Entfaltung; *SOFI Mitteilungen* 28: 103–112.
Schütz, Alfred (1944): The Stranger: An Essay in Social Psychology; *American Journal of Sociology* 49: 499-507.
Schütze, Fritz (1983): Biographieforschung und Narratives Interview; *Neue Praxis* 13(3): 283–293.
Scott, James C. (1985): *Weapons of the Weak – Everyday Forms of Peasant Resistance*; New Haven: Yale University Press.
Seamon, David (1980): Body-subject, Time Space Routines and Place Ballets; In: Buttimer, Anne and Seamon, David (eds.). *The Human Experience of Space and Place*. pp. 148–165. New York: St. Martins Press.
Sennett, Richard (1978): *The Fall of Public Man*; London: Faber.
Sennett, Richard (1998): *The Corrosion of Character. The Personal Consequences of Work in the New Capitalism*; New York: Norton.
Sennett, Richard and Cobb, Jonathan (1972): *The Hidden Injuries of Class*; New York and London: Norton.
Sharp, Joanne (2009): Geography and genDer: What Belongs to Feminist Geography? Emotion, Power and Change; *Progress in Human Geography* 33(1): 74–80.
Sharpe, Scott (2013): The Aesthetics of Urban Movement: Habits, Mobility, and Resistance; *Geographical Research* 51(2): 166–172.
Simmel, Georg (1971a [1908]): The Stranger; In: Levine, Donald N. (ed.). *Georg Simmel On Individuality and Social Form*. pp. 143–150. Chicago: University of Chicago Press.
Simmel, Georg (1971b [1903]): The Metropolis and Mental Life; In: Levine, Donald N. (ed.). *Georg Simmel On Individuality and Social Form*. pp. 324–339. Chicago: University of Chicago Press.
Skeggs, Beverley (2004): *Class, Self, Culture*; London: Routledge.
Smith, Allison E. (2009): *Ageing in Urban Neighbourhoods. Place Attachment and Social Exclusion*; Bristol: Policy Press.
Smith, Neil (1996): *The New Urban Frontier. Gentrification and the Revanchist City*; London: Routledge.
Sorkin, Michael (1992): *Variations on a Theme Park. The New American City and the End of Public Space*; New York: Hill and Wong.
Stacey, Margaret (1969): The Myths of Community Studies; *British Journal of Sociology* 20(2): 134–147.
Stadt Nürnberg (1977; 1980; 2007; 2015; 2018): Statistische Jahrbücher der Stadt Nürnberg, Amt für Stadtforschung und Statistik, Nürnberg.
Stadt Nürnberg (2007): Wirtschaftsreferat, Nürnberg.
Stadt Nürnberg (2009): Wirtschaftsbericht 49, Nürnberg.
Stadt Nürnberg (2011a): *Statistischer Monatsbericht für Juni 2011*; Nürnberg.
Stadt Nürnberg (2011b): *Menschen mit Migrationshintergrund in Nürnberg*; Nürnberg: Amt für Stadtforschung und Statistik.
Stadt Nürnberg (2013): http://www.nuernberg.de/internet/portal/wirtschaft /struktur.html (accessed 18th May 2013).
Stadt Nürnberg (2015): *Statistischer Monatsbericht für November 2014- Sozialraumtypisierung für Nürnberg*; Nürnberg: Amt für Stadtforschung und Statistik.
Stadt Nürnberg (2018a): *Datenblatt Migrationshintergrund Nürnberg Statistischer Bezirk: 46 Werderau*; Nürnberg: Amt für Stadtforschung und Statistik.

Stadt Nürnberg (2018b): *Kindertagesbetreuung 2008 bis 2017 in Nürnberg und Fürth; Statistischer Monatsbericht. 28.5.2018.* Nürnberg: Amt für Stadtforschung und Statistik.

Stadt Nürnberg (2019a): *Sozialversicherungspflichtig Beschäftigte nach Geschlecht. Statistisches Infosystem Nürnberg.* Statistisches Landesamt. https://online-service2.nuernberg.de/aswn/ASW.exe?aw=MBES_J03 (accessed 6.2.2019).

Stadt Nürnberg (2019b): *Statistisches Jahrbuch der Stadt Nürnberg 2018*; Nürnberg: Amt für Stadtforschung und Statistik.

Stadt Nürnberg (2019c): *Nürnberg in Zahlen 2019*; Nürnberg: Amt für Stadtforschung und Statistik.

Stake, Robert E. (2000): Case Studies; In: Denzin, Norman K. and Lincoln, Yvonna S. (eds.). *Handbook of Qualitative Research.* pp. 435–454. London: Sage.

Statistisches Bundesamt (2018): *Statistisches Jahrbuch 2018*; Wiesbaden.

Stewart, Kathleen (1988): Nostalgia—A Polemic; *Cultural Anthropology* 3(3): 227–241.

Storm, Anna (2014): *Post-Industrial Landscape Scars*; Houndsmills: Palgrave Macmillan.

Strangleman, Tim (2007): The Nostalgia for Permanence at Work? The End of Work and its Commentators; *The Sociologica Review* 55(1): 81–102.

Strangleman, Tim (2012): Work Identity in Crisis? Rethinking the Problem of Attachment and Loss at Work; *Sociology* 46(3): 411–425.

Strangleman, Tim (2014): Remembering Working-Class Life. History, Sociology and Working Class Studies; *Sociology* 48(6): 1232–1237.

Strauss, Anselm and Corbin, Juliet (1994): Grounded Theory Methodology. An Overview; In: Denzin, Norman K. and Lincoln, Yvonna S. (eds.). *Handbook of Qualitative Research.* pp. 273–285. Thousand Oaks: Sage.

Süddeutsche Zeitung (2011): Kluge Köpfe für starke Marken – Nürnberg wandelt sich zaghaft von einer Arbeiter zu einer Akademikerstadt; Süddeutsche Zeitung. 11./12.September. München: V2/11.

Taylor, Ian; Evans, Karen and Fraser, Penny (1996): *A Tale of Two Cities. Global Change, local feeling and everyday life in the North of England. A Study in Manchester and Sheffield*; London: Routledge.

Taylor, Nicholas (1973): *The Village in the City*; London: Maurice Temple Smith.

Taylor, Yvette (2012): *Fitting into Place?* Aldershot: Ashgate.

Theodossopoulos, Dimitrios (2013): Infuriated with the Infuriated? Blaming Tactics and Discontent about the Greek Financial Crisis; *Current Anthropology* 54(2): 200–221.

Thiel, Darren (2012): *Builders: Class, Gender and Ethnicity in the Construction Industry*; London: Routledge.

Thien, Deborah (2005): After or Beyond Feeling? A Consideration of Affect and Emotion in Geography; *Area* 37(4): 450–454.

Thompson, Edward Palmer (1963): *The Making of the English Working Class*; Harmondsworth: Penguin.

Thompson, Edward Palmer (1978): *The Poverty of Theory and Other Essays*; London: Merlin.

Till, Karen (2005): *The New Berlin: Memory, Politics, Place*; Minneapolis, MN: University of Minnesota Press.

Till, Karen (2008): Artistic and Activist Memory Work. Approaching Place-based Practice; *Memory Studies* 1(1): 99–113.

Trigg, Dylan (2009): The Place of Trauma. Memory, Hauntings and the Temporality of Ruins; *Memory Studies* 2(1): 87–101.

Tuan, Yi-Fu (1977): *Space and Place. The Perspective of Experience*; Minneapolis: University of Minnesota Press.

Tuan, Yi-Fu (2004): Senses of Place – Its Relationship to Self and Time; In: Mels, Tom (ed.). *Reanimating Places – A Geography of Rhythms*. pp. 45–55. Aldershot: Ashgate.

Urry, John and Larsen, Jonas (2011): *The Tourist Gaze 3.0*; London: Sage.

Valentine, Gill (1989): The Geography of Women's Fear; *Area* 21: 385–390.

Valentine, Gill (2008): Living with Difference. Reflections on Geographies of encounter; *Progress in Human Geography* 32: 323–337.

Valentine, Gill and McKendrick, John (1997): Children's Outdoor Play: Exploring Parental Concerns about Children's Safety and the Changing Nature of Childhood; *Geoforum* 28(2): 219–235.

Vanolo, Alberto (2008): The Image of the Creative City: Some Reflections on Urban Branding in Turin; *Cities* 25: 370–382.

Vertovec, Steven (2007): Super-diversity and its Implications; *Ethnic and Racial Studies* 29(6): 1024–1054.

Vertovec, Steven and Wessendorf, Susanne (eds.) (2010): *The Multiculturalism Backlash. European Discourses, Policies and Practices*; London: Routledge.

Vogel, Berthold (2010): Wohlstandskonflikte und Unsicherheitsverschärfung. Die Mitte der Gesellschaft gerät unter Druck; In: Soeffner, Hans-Georg (ed.). *Unsichere Zeiten. Herausforderungen gesellschaftlicher Transformationen*. pp. 157–168. Wiesbaden: VS Verlag.

Voiculescu, Sorina and Jucu, Ioan Sebastian (2016): Producing Urban Industrial Derelict Places: The Case of the Solventul Petrochemical Plant in Timişoara; *European Urban and Regional Studies* 23(4): 765–781.

Walkerdine, Valerie (2010): Communal Beingness and Affect – An Exploration of Trauma in an Ex-industrial Community; *Body & Society* 16(1): 91–116.

Ware, Vron (2008): Towards a Sociology of Resentment. A Debate on Class and Whiteness; *Sociological Research Online* 13(5): 9.

Watson, Sophie (2006): *City Publics. The (Dis)Enchantments of Urban Encounters*; London: Routledge.

Weber, Max (2015 [1904/1905]): *Die protestantische Ethik und der Geist des Kapitalismus*; Berlin: Hofenberg.

Wessendorf, Susanne (2013): Commonplace Diversity and the 'Ethos of Mixing': Perceptions of Difference in a London Neighbourhood; *Identities* 20(4): 407–422.

West, Candace and Zimmerman, Don H. (1987): Doing Gender; *Gender & Society* 1: 125–151.

Weyrather, Irmgard (2003): *Die Frau am Fließband – Das Bild der Fabrikarbeiterin in der Sozialforschung 1870–1985*; Frankfurt a.M.: Campus Verlag.

Wheeler, Rebecca (2014): Mining Memories in a Rural Community: Landscape, Temporality and Place Identity; *Journal of Rural Studies* 36: 22–32.

Wheeler, Rebecca (2017): Local History as Productive Nostalgia? Change, Continuity and Sense of Place in Rural England; *Social & Cultural Geography* 18(4): 466–486.

Wiles, Janine L.; Allen, Ruth E. S.; Palmer, Anthea J.; Hayman, Karen J.; Keeling, Sally and Kerse, Ngaire (2009): Older People and their Social Spaces: A Study of

well-being and Attachment to Place in Aotearoa; *Social Science & Medicine* 68(4): 664–671.
Wiley, John (2007): The spectral geographies of W.G. Sebald; *Cultural Geographies* 14: 171–188.
Willems, Herbert (1997): *Rahmen und Habitus. Zum theoretischen und methodischen Ansatz Erving Goffmans. Vergleiche, Anschlüsse und Anwendungen*; Frankfurt a.M.: Suhrkamp.
Williams, Claire (1993): Class, Gender and the Body. The Occupational Health and Safety Concerns of Blue Collar Workers in the South Asian Timer Industry; In: Quinlan, Michael (ed.). *Work and Health. The Origins, Management and Regulation of Occupational Illness*. Melbourne: Macmillan.
Williams, Raymond (1965 [1961]): *The Long Revolution*; Harmondsworth: Penguin.
Williams, Raymond (1973): *The Country and the City*; London: Chatto and Windus.
Williams, Raymond (1977): *Marxism and Literature*; Oxford: Oxford University Press.
Williams, Raymond (1979 [1958]): *Culture and Society 1780–1959*; Harmondsworth: Penguin.
Willis, Paul (1977): *Learning to Labour – How Working Class Kids Get Working Class Jobs*; Farnborough: Saxon House.
Wilson, Helen F. (2011): Passing Propinquities in the Multicultural City: The Everyday Encounters of Bus Passengering; *Environment and Planning A* 43: 634–649.
Wimmer, Andreas (2004): Does Ethnicity Matter? Everyday Group Formation in Three Swiss Immigrant Neighbourhoods; *Ethnic and Racial Studies* 27(1): 1–36.
Winker, Gabriele and Degele, Nina (2009): *Intersektionalität. Zur Analyse sozialer Ungleichheiten*; Bielefeld: Transcript.
Wise, Amanda and Velayutham, Selvaraj (eds.) (2009): *Everyday Multiculturalism*; Houndsmills: Palgrave Macmillan.
Wolff, Friedrich (2012): *Gartenstädte in und um Berlin*; Berlin: Bäßler.
Woodward, Kath; Muriji, Karim; Neal, Sarah and Watson, Sophie (2014): Class Debate; *Sociology* 48(3): 427–428.
World Bank (2020): GINI Index (World Bank estimate) – Germany, United Kingdom; https://data.worldbank.org/indicator/SI.POV.GINI?end=2016&locations=DE-GB&name_desc=true&start=1969&view=chart (Accessed on 31 August 2020)
Wright, Erik Olin (1997): *Class Counts – Comparative Studies in Class Analysis*; Cambridge: Cambridge University Press.
Wylie, John (2007): *Landscape*; London: Routledge.
Wylie, John (2009): Landscape, Absence and the Geographies of love; *Transactions of the Institute of British Geographers* 34: 275–289.
Yin, Robert K. (2003): *Case Study Research Design and Methods*; Thousand Oaks: Sage.
Yodanis, Carrie (2006): A Place in Town: Doing Class in a Coffee Shop; *Journal of Contemporary Ethnography* 35(3): 341–366.
Young, Michael and Willmott, Peter (1957): *Family and Kinship in East London*; London: Routledge.
Yuk-Ha Tsang, Eileen (2014): *The New Middle Class in China. Consumption, Politics and the Market Economy*; Basingstoke: Palgrave Macmillan.
Yuval-Davis, Nira (2006): Intersectionality and Feminist Politics; *European Journal of Women's Studies* 13(3): 193–209.

Zelizer, Barbie (1995): Reading the Past against the Grain: The Shape of Memory Studies; *Critical Studies in Mass Communication* 12: 214–239.
Zerubavel, Eviatar (1996): Social Memories. Steps to a Sociology of the Past; *Qualitative Sociology* 19(3): 283–299.
Zerubavel, Eviatar (2003): *Time Maps: Collective Memory and the Social Shape of the Past*; Chicago: University of Chicago Press.
Zhang, Li and Zhao, Simon Xiaobin (2009): City Branding and the Olympic Effect: A Case Study of Beijing; *Cities* 26: 245–254.
Žižek, Slavoj (2012): *The Year of Dreaming Dangerously*; London: Verso.
Zukin, Sharon (1982): *Loft Living – Culture and Capital in Urban Change*; Baltimore: John Hopkins University Press.
Zukin, Sharon (1993): *Landscapes of Power. From Detroit to Disney World*; Berkeley: University of California Press.
Zukin, Sharon (2011): *Naked City – The Death and Life of Authentic Urban Places*; Oxford: Oxford University Press.

Index

For Product Safety Concerns and Information please contact our EU representative GPSR@taylorandfrancis.com
Taylor & Francis Verlag GmbH, Kaufingerstraße 24, 80331 München, Germany

www.ingramcontent.com/pod-product-compliance
Ingram Content Group UK Ltd.
Pitfield, Milton Keynes, MK11 3LW, UK
UKHW020002200926
475702UK00015B/2431
* 9 7 8 0 3 6 7 7 7 5 0 2 5 *